EMBRACING FITNESS

Michael R. Slavit, Ph.D.

ISBN - 13: 978-1536936551
ISBN - 10:   1536936553

Library of Congress Control Number: 2016913682
CreateSpace Independent Publishing Platform
North Charleston, South Carolina

Embracing Fitness

Exercise: Why and How

Michael R. Slavit, Ph.D., ABPP
Board Certified in Behavioral and Cognitive Psychology
with two chapters by
Chris Crawford, Fitness Instructor

Table of Contents

Introduction

For whom is this book intended?

This book is intended for you if:

- You have been reluctant to start a fitness routine.

- You have a fitness routine that is feeling stale.

- You have a history of starting fitness routines, but abandoning them because they felt unpleasant or difficult.

- You want to know about the various types of exercise and their advantages.

- You want to know more about how exercise fits in with other aspects of health maintenance.

What will I learn from this book?

There are many reasons to stay fit, and the advantages of fitness will be discussed. Among the advantages of being fit are better resistance to disease, improved memory and concentration, improved self-esteem and, very importantly, better ability to rebound from injury or illness.

There will be an emphasis on helping the reader to realize that exercise is **not**, in and of itself, unpleasant. The thoughts and judgments we make about exercise will determine whether we experience exercise as pleasant or unpleasant.

There is reason to believe, from an evolutionary standpoint, that we are the descendants of people who tolerated a vigorous lifestyle without complaint.

The reader will be introduced to six categories of exercise:

- Strength training
- Aerobic training
- Balance training
- Flexibility training
- Mind-body integration
- Core stability training

You will be introduced to all six types of exercise. Although some specific exercises will be described and illustrated regarding care of the back, care of the shoulders, and a few yoga and Pilates exercises, this is not basically a "how to" book. There are many sources of information on specific exercises, and the reference section lists a number of them. Even when specific exercises are not illustrated, such with regard to strength training and stretching, you will nonetheless be introduced to a number of important concepts regarding these subjects.

One point that will be made repeatedly throughout this book is that the best exercise routine for you is the one you do not dread. You will be challenged to try to experience exercise as vigorous, vital and pleasant. However, if you cannot accomplish this with a particular type of exercise, there is little advantage in trying to do it. You will eventually, probably sooner rather than later, drop a routine that you cannot learn to enjoy. You are much more likely to persist with the program you do not dread.

There is a chapter entitled "Refuel and Recover after Exercise." Contrary to popular belief, carbohydrates are recommended immediately after a workout, with a high protein meal within an hour and a half afterward.

There are chapters entitled "Care of your Back" and "Care of your Shoulders." Specific exercises are described and illustrated in these chapters. However, you are advised to consult with a physician and a physical therapist before embarking on a program in these areas, especially if you have any discomfort or injury in them.

Contributing author Chris Crawford, fitness instructor, has provided a chapter describing her personal journey of using exercise, fitness and a strong mental attitude to recover from a medical challenge. Chris also has a chapter describing the power fitness has had to transform the lives of some of her students.

There is a chapter entitled, "Can't I just make it fun?" Many individuals will only exercise if it is part of fun and games. Still others will only exercise if they have a partner with whom to work out. In both of these instances the individuals will exercise only if they can distract themselves from the fact of exercise. Although it is better to exercise at a game or with a partner than to not exercise at all, there is danger in such a requirement. Games and partners may be unavailable, and the exercise regimen can be abandoned. It is preferable to "stare down any resistance" you have to exercise. This point has been previously stated, but is worth re-emphasizing. There is nothing, in and of itself, about exercise that is unpleasant. There is reason to believe that we are the descendants of people who at least tolerated, and probably enjoyed, strenuous physical activity. You have the ability to change your attitude about exercise, and to learn to experience it as vital and enjoyable rather than as arduous and unpleasant. I am issuing a challenge to you, gentle reader, to adopt this attitude about exercise if you have not done so already. The benefits are well worth it!

There is a section on "Overall Health Maintenance." Fitness is not just a matter of exercise, but also requires adequate nutrition, good sleep habits and a good mental attitude. Specific recommendations will be made in these key areas.

There is a chapter entitled "The Motivation Factor," in which motivation is broken down into six components. Viewing motivation in light of these factors may help you increase your effective motivation rather than to view motivation as something over which you have limited control.

There is also a chapter encouraging you to keep your fitness regimen in its proper perspective. Fitness is best seen as being "in service of" other life goals. It is important to be sure the fitness regimen itself does not become more important than the life goals it serves. Finally, you are encouraged to "Embrace Life and Fitness" with what I hope are words of inspiration. Science has given us understanding of how the Universe has made our existence possible. Life is a gift and an opportunity best not squandered. *A vital and happy life is more easily attained with fitness than without it.* Read with an open mind and make fitness a regular part of Your lifestyle.

Chapter 1
The Fitness Obsession

The best-designed workout in the world
will not help you if you avoid it.

Staying fit is a national obsession. Some individuals obsess about how to improve their fitness regimen. Some individuals obsess about how arduous and unpleasant their fitness routine feels to them. Some persons want to begin an exercise program and obsess over when and where to begin. Still others have no intention to exercise, but obsess over the health implications of their inactivity. Any way you cut it, fitness is a national obsession.

If President John F. Kennedy were alive today, he might be discouraged by some of the aspects of American culture that he would see. But one thing he would be very proud of is the emphasis in American society, at least among a portion of the population, on physical fitness. Fitness has become a strong theme among many persons in our culture. Sometime in the

1980's, jogging suits and running shoes became proper attire for many public places other than athletic facilities. Women's athletics have taken their place along with men's (It is illegal in public education to ignore women's athletics in favor of men's in terms of spending of tax dollars). The ideal of female beauty, once a softer, less athletic one than that for men, has changed. In countless ways, we are showing that physical fitness is important to us.

Exercise has become recognized as a legitimate preventative measure for such conditions as hypertension, type II Diabetes and heart disease. Research in the field of immunology has shown that physical exercise can enhance the effectiveness of the human immune system. Exercise is sometimes referred to as "America's best arthritis medicine." And, very importantly, there is growing evidence that exercise slows down, and to a degree even reverses, the cognitive problems that can arise with aging.

There are many popular forms of exercise, but I do not intend to help you choose an exercise program. Your own age, level of fitness, tastes, lifestyle, and physical limitations will guide you. There are a number of professionals in physical education, physical therapy, chiropractic, osteopathy, and orthopedics to turn to if you want help in planning a training regimen. My first goal is to help you develop a positive attitude toward exercise and fitness. Next, my intentions are to encourage you to establish a fitness program, and to help you carry out the one you choose.

The best-designed workout in the world will not help you if you avoid it. This may appear to be a simple minded assertion, but years of experience working with people has impressed me with how often people miss their workouts. And most of the missed workouts are due not to illness, injury, or any unavoidable cause, but rather to emotional and behavioral causes.

A Matter of Feeling, Perception and Cognitive Maps

One very frequent cause of individuals abandoning their fitness regimen is any change in the normal flow of their daily lives. The following are some of the changes that have this unfortunate result:

- Change of job.

- Moving from one house or apartment to another.

- The approach of a major holiday.

- Preparation for an event such as a family member's wedding, graduation, et cetera.

I believe that the abandonment of a fitness regimen under the circumstances listed above is actually a problem of perception, feeling or cognitive mapping. As I have been writing this section, gentle reader, I am aware that the concept is somewhat fuzzy and difficult to convey. Nonetheless, I believe it is important. It may be worth your while to read this short section twice to get a good sense for it.

A cognitive map is an internal representation of space or time. If we have a daily routine that we typically follow, there is, whether you are consciously aware of it or not, some type of visual representation of this in your mind. If the internal visual representation of your daily activities has a space in it for a workout, you are more likely to engage in the activity. When there is an unusual event such as one of those I listed above, the cognitive map may be cluttered or dismantled. In reality, whether we are packing to move, starting a new job, or planning for an event, there probably is time for three workouts per week if the workouts are a priority to us and if we think it through clearly. However, if we do not think pointedly and clearly about it, our perception of the coming days or weeks may have "a cluttered feel to it" when we access our obligations in our minds. A cluttered or dismantled cognitive map can result in a felt sense that one's tasks and obligations are excessive, or even overwhelming.

The feeling or perception that one may have at such a time is that there is no time for exercise. The exercise regimen is thus abandoned. Despite the perception, or the felt sense, that no time exists for a workout, in many cases the reality is that the exercise routine could be worked in and maintained.

Of course, I am writing about obligations imposed by such situations as moving, a job change, or event planning. There are situations such as illness or injury to oneself or a loved one that could truly monopolize one's time and preclude an exercise regimen. However, it will be in your interest to think clearly about these situations and to do your best to clear away any feelings or perceptions that could unnecessarily crowd out exercise and fitness.

Purposes of this Book

- To describe some of the advantages of exercise,
- To describe some of the different forms of exercise that are beneficial to our bodies and minds.
- To explain some of the ways we can abandon a fitness program.
- To promote a philosophy of moderation that can enable you to successfully and permanently integrate exercise into your lifetime regimen.
- To help you accept that exercise can be enjoyable and not drudgery.
- To promote the idea of fitness as a combination of exercise, good nutrition, sleep and a strong mental attitude, and
- To strongly encourage you to revel in the gift of life and to enhance your ability to derive joy and contentment in life through nutrition, sleep, a strong mental attitude and exercise.

Chapter 2
Why Stay Fit?

*Your muscle tissue can literally grow more capillaries
to supply the blood and oxygen needed
to sustain an increased demand.*

Staying Well

The human immune system is a very complicated entity. It has been observed that our immune system employs the most diverse workforce ever assembled. Although we have fewer than twenty-five thousand coding genes, we have over a million antibodies ready to fight off invading antigens. However, our immune system's effectiveness can be compromised in a number of ways, including insufficient sleep, poor nutrition, anxiety, depression, and physical inactivity.

Remaining Generally Capable after Illness or Injury

A general principle in the area of fitness, aerobic training and strength training is "stress and adaptation." Our muscles and our lung capacity tend to build themselves to be adequate to handle the amount of stress placed on them. This is the basis of most physical training. If you think about it, gentle reader, you will realize how obvious this is.

Let us assume you knew you were going on an excursion that was going to require you to walk two miles, and that you had been very inactive. You may go for a walk and find that after a half-mile you are exhausted and gasping for breath. Therefore, every day for three weeks you go for a daily walk, and on every fourth day you increase your distance by one-quarter mile. Therefore, for three days you walk one-half mile. On the fourth day, you add one-quarter mile, making your walk three-quarters of a mile. On the seventh day, you begin walking one full mile, and so forth. By the time you reach three weeks you are walking two full miles.

Most persons would agree that such a program would work, but few actually think through the reason. The reason is that you are gradually increasing the stress to which you are subjecting your heart, lungs and legs; and your heart, lungs and legs are adapting to the stress placed on them. Your muscle tissue can literally grow more capillaries to supply the blood and oxygen needed to sustain an increased demand.

So, what does this have to do with remaining generally capable after injury or disease? Well, let us suppose that you have no physical fitness program in effect. You get out of bed, attend to hygiene, get in and out of chairs, walk short distances to and from your car, operate a keyboard, handle a cooking pot and a serving spoon, et cetera. Essentially, you perform your Activities of Daily Living (hereafter referred to simply as ADLs). Your body will therefore adapt to the performance of your ADLs. You will have the strength and stamina to perform your ADLs, but little more.

If you sustained an injury or contracted a disease that kept you in bed and off your feet for a month, your body's muscles would experience decay due to lack of use. This decay is known as atrophy. After a month in bed, you might be pronounced cured, and you would get up and attempt to resume your normal range of activities. However, you might find you lack the strength and stamina to get through your day. Why would this be so? The reason is that in living your normal daily life, you may have developed perhaps only 120% of the strength and stamina needed to conduct your ADLs. When you were ill and off your feet for a month, you could perhaps have lost 33% of your strength and stamina. This would leave you with only eighty percent of the strength and stamina you need to get through your daily activities, leaving you unable to persist through the day.

However, with a regular, moderate fitness regimen, it is not unusual for individuals to develop three or four times the strength and stamina needed for their ADLs. If an individual with 300% of the strength needed for normal daily activities were to lose 33% of their strength during an illness, that individual would, after the illness, still have twice as much strength as needed to persist at ADLs through a day. Thus, it is in our better interest to maintain an exercise regimen to ensure our ability to recover from injury or disease.

Health and Longevity

In his book *The Exercise Cure*, Dr. Jordan Metzl described a medical journal report on a study of more than 600,000 people. The study showed that persons who exercised 2.5 hours per week increased their life expectancy by 3.5 years. In addition, subjects in the study who exercised more intensively increased their life expectancy by 4.2 years.

Dr. Metzl describes the following benefits of regular exercise:

- Research has shown that exercise can reduce the progression of type-2 diabetes by 58 percent.
- Exercise reduces blood pressure and cholesterol, thereby lessening the chances of heart attack and stroke.
- Exercise boosts our immune response against such maladies as cold and flu.
- Exercise has been shown to reduce symptoms of depression by thirty percent.
- Exercise increases bone density. Postmenopausal women who exercised four times per week had a forty-seven percent lower risk of hip fractures.
- Exercise helps reduce chronic inflammation in the body. Since chronic, low-level inflammation is implicated in such very serious problems as heart disease, arthritis, Alzheimer's Disease, Parkinson's Disease and asthma, the health advantages of exercise cannot be overstated.

Unexpected Benefits of Exercise

Exercise can promote life enhancing benefits in ways that are not even planned. In a study published in 2006 in the British Journal of Health Psychology, sedentary individuals were put on an exercise program. Without being asked to do so, participants reported that they:

- Smoked less.
- Used fewer alcoholic and caffeinated drinks.
- Made healthier food choices.
- Did more household chores.
- Made less frequent use of their credit cards, and
- Were more diligent at study and work obligations.

Dr. Todd Heatherton, professor of psychology and brain sciences at Dartmouth College, explains this result by stating, "Regular exercise builds self-regulatory resources." Let us put that in day-to-day terms. When we do not exercise, we will have unconscious feelings of discomfort. Our bodies have not been put to their natural, energetic use, and we will have an internal sense of tension or fidgetiness. This can be translated into a felt sense that there is a hole that needs to be filled or an itch to be scratched. How do we fill that hole or scratch that unconscious itch? We may smoke, drink, eat sweet or fatty snacks, buy an unnecessary treat or lie down to take a break. When we exercise, we feel better physically. We are *not* as likely to have that felt sense of a hole to be filled or an itch to be scratched. We are more likely to feel better and attend to study, work or household tasks. We are less likely to indulge in unneeded spending or unhealthy habits, and we are less likely to feel the need to escape by lying down. Exercise leads to healthier, more vital living.

Exercise and the Brain

There is an ever-growing body of evidence that exercise is important not only for the functioning of your heart, muscles and internal organs, but also for the functioning of your brain. This should not be surprising, as the brain is part of your body and receives its nutrients through the bloodstream just as do your heart, lungs, liver, and kidneys. In *Magnificent at Any Age*, Dr. Daniel Amon writes,

> Being a physical slug is bad for your brain, even if you are spending all of your time doing crossword puzzles. The brain needs physical exercise. Without it, the brain struggles. Exercise boosts blood to the brain, which helps supply oxygen, glucose and other nutrients and takes away toxic substances. If the deep areas of the brain are starved of healthy blood flow, you will have problems with coordination and processing complex thoughts.

In a 2014 article in the journal *Sports Medicine*, researchers Emily Zhao and others reported on the effects of exercise on the maintenance of cognitive ability in aging adults. They stated that only thirty percent of aging is based on genetics, while seventy percent is based on lifestyle. They concluded:

> Evidence suggests that maintaining a high level of cardiopulmonary fitness and mobility exhibits protective effects on structural changes that occur with aging in areas of the brain associated with memory, attention, and task completion. Chronic exercise is also associated with preservation of overall cognitive functioning and prevention of dementia.

Another 2014 report in Sports Medicine, by Romain Meeusen, indicated:

> Accumulating evidence suggests that diet and lifestyle can play an important role in delaying the onset or halting the progression of age-related health disorders and can improve cognitive function. Exercise has been promoted as a possible prevention for neuro-degenerative diseases.

In particular, Meeusen cited evidence that regular exercise resulted in a two percent increase in the size of the brain structure called the hippocampus, known to be an integral part of memory function. He stated that this volume increase "effectively reverses age-related losses in volume by 1-2 years."

Meeusen also states,

> There is now ample evidence that physical activity decreases the incidence of cardiovascular disease,

colon and breast cancer, and obesity, and also diseases such as Alzheimer's, depression, and anxiety.

Jennifer Davis et al. reported the following in the British Journal of Sports Medicine:

> Cognitive decline is one of the most prominent healthcare issues of the 21st century. Within the context of combating cognitive decline through behavioral interventions, physical activity is a promising approach.

The list of studies goes on. Let it suffice for our purposes here to state that evidence is accumulating that brain function is positively influenced by exercise, and that regular exercise slows down the aging process.

The benefits of exercise are immense. Despite this, a huge percentage of people have experienced difficulty starting or persisting with an exercise routine due to a feeling that exercise is and must always be difficult, arduous and unpleasant. If that is your belief, one purpose of this book is to help you to overcome it. You will be asked to suspend that belief in order to establish more realistic and helpful thinking. You will be asked, while exercising, to tell yourself that the activity feels energetic, vital and good. The next chapter will emphasize that idea.

Chapter 3
It is Not Unpleasant

*I think it is fair to say that enjoyment of physical
activity exists in our genetic heritage and
resides deep within our psyche.*

Doctors Diane Dahm and Jay Smith, authors of *The Mayo
Clinic: Fitness for Everybody*, ask the following:

> Imagine that a new wonder drug has been created. It
> will help prevent illness and disease – including
> cancer. It will help you lose excess weight, and keep it
> off. It will slow the aging process, making you look
> and feel younger than your years. It will give you
> energy and increase your self-esteem. It will reduce
> stress, fight depression and anxiety, and put you in a
> better mood. It will make you stronger and healthier.
> It will improve your posture, your flexibility, your
> balance and your endurance. It will even help you
> sleep better. Sounds appealing, doesn't it? This
> miracle drug is available right now, and you can start
> taking it today. It is called exercise.

I believe that most people today recognize that exercise
would be beneficial. Nevertheless, many still find it
extremely difficult to establish exercise as a habit. The
primary reason people fail to maintain an exercise regimen is

their perception that exercise is unpleasant, laborious, onerous, and arduous.

There is nothing about exercise that is, in and of itself, arduous or unpleasant.

The fact is that there is nothing about exercise that is, in and of itself, arduous or unpleasant. In fact, it is quite likely that enjoyment of physical activity is part of our genetic heritage. Just think about it. Our ancestors had to migrate to find food, gather and hunt food, defend themselves and their offspring from predators, and create shelters. Most of our ancestors undoubtedly had to lead very physically active and demanding lives. Those who did not enjoy heavy physical activity, and therefore did it with less vigor or commitment, were less likely to survive, reproduce, and successfully protect their offspring. Their genes were less likely to be passed on to future generations. Therefore, I think it is fair to say that enjoyment of physical activity exists in our genetic heritage and resides deep within our psyche.

Change Your Mind to Change Your Experience

Assume for a moment that you are beginning to exercise by getting on a treadmill and doing brisk walking. If you tell yourself, "This is difficult. This is arduous. This is unpleasant," you will definitely dislike the experience, and you will probably stop exercising at the first excuse. Alternatively, if you get on the same treadmill and tell yourself, "This feels vigorous. This feels vital. This feels good." you may well find yourself enjoying the experience. You will be much less likely to be derailed from your fitness regimen.

Your body-mind system is ready to learn to enjoy exercise.
You have to make up your mind to be open
to feelings of enjoyment

If you want to enjoy the benefits of physical fitness, you will have to challenge the belief that physical exercise is arduous, unpleasant and too demanding to be enjoyed. You will have to teach yourself to love the feelings of strenuous physical exercise. Your body-mind system is ready to learn to enjoy exercise. All you have to make up your mind to be open to those feelings of enjoyment.

Avoiding Pitfalls and Maintaining Your Fitness Routine

Once you have changed your mind about exercise and have taught yourself to enjoy it, the threats to a consistent routine have not passed. It sometimes happens that a person will establish an exercise routine, and will then become so ardent that the routine becomes difficult to maintain.

Kim's account may be a good illustration:

I love to stay fit. I just love it. And I have always liked to push myself to higher levels of fitness. My main activities are running, weight lifting and softball. Softball is just for fun, but running and weight lifting are serious training for me. However, they are not quite as serious as they used to be and, because of that, I'm doing better at them than ever before.

Before I learned to manage things better, I used to be very rigid about always making my workouts tougher and never backing off. For example, when I started running for fitness at age 22, I used to jog a mile, and I did not time it. I began to wonder how long it took me, so I brought a watch along. In retrospect, that was a big mistake! I first timed myself at seven minutes and forty-five seconds for the mile. I kept bringing the watch to see how I would do as I continued to train. After a while, I saw it as a challenge for me to do better than I had the day before. Within two months, I had my time for the mile down to 6:30, and I was sure I would be running the mile in under 6:00 very soon.

Then, one day I was not feeling very well. I was not actually sick, just a little tired. I thought about how much energy I had to expend to run the mile in six minutes, and I could not handle the idea, so I just skipped it altogether. That became the pattern. I was afraid to do my running on days when I did not feel my very best, because I was afraid of "running a bad time." In addition, even when I felt fine physically, I still dreaded the run because of the pressure I was putting on myself.

Finally, it was explained to me what I was doing to myself. I was doing my running less often, and I was not enjoying it at all. With some encouragement, I totally dropped the idea of timing. I have not brought a watch with me since then. If I am feeling particularly strong and enthusiastic, I run harder, but I do not care about the actual time. If I am not feeling my best, I run more slowly. But I do my running anyway, since there is no pressure to meet any standard. I am in better condition than ever, and I enjoy the activity again.

Kim's story illustrates a very important point for individuals who want to keep up an exercise program for fitness. You may want to measure your performance, and to improve in some way. That may serve as a helpful motivator, but there are dangers involved. First, you may lose your intrinsic enjoyment of the activity due to the pressure you put on yourself to improve. Second, you could easily begin to dread your exercise routine, and to avoid it. You will be much more physically fit if you establish a moderate exercise routine and perform it regularly than if you establish a more demanding routine and avoid it frequently.

Phil has a story that will also be instructive:

> I love to work out to stay in shape. I do some bicycling and brisk walking, but my main activity is weight training. I belong to a fitness center, and I go there three times a week to work out. My workouts are enjoyable, but it was not always that way.
>
> I started with a workout that consisted of twenty sets of exercises and that took me approximately 45 minutes. I stayed with this basic workout for several months, the only change being that I increased the amount of weight I was lifting on a few exercises. Then I had a few days in which I felt particularly strong and energetic, and I doubled up on a few exercises, bringing my total workout to 26 sets and approximately an hour. Once I had done this a few times, I decided I should stick with the expanded routine. I even added 2 sets each of 2 new

exercises, bringing my session to 30 sets and an hour and twenty minutes.

I was really excited about the progress I was making, but it didn't last. I had made my routine so difficult that on my less energetic days I would dread going to the fitness center. I began to miss workouts every time I had an excuse to do so. I started to feel guilty about the whole affair. Then I was encouraged to try a different approach to my fitness sessions. First, I cut my routine back down to the original 20 sets, which took me about 45 minutes. Second, I told myself that if I felt really energetic for a day, a week, or even several weeks, I would allow myself to expand my workout during that period of high energy. But, I would revert to the 20-set workout the very first time I found myself dreading the workout or finding it unpleasant and burdensome. Third, I decided that if I started my routine and it felt tiresome and unpleasant instead of fun and rewarding, I would give myself permission to cut the workout short, shower, and leave.

After I had made these decisions, I continued with the 20-set workout for several weeks. Then I had an energetic period. I expanded the workout to 24 sets for two weeks. During my first workout of the third week, it began to feel tiresome, and I cut the session to 20 sets that very day. I did not "find any excuses" to miss any sessions the way I had in the past whenever I had expanded my routine. As far as giving myself permission to cut the workout short and leave early, I have used that only once, but it makes a big difference. I never dread the workout because I know I can allow myself to cut it short if it feels burdensome. I am more confident than ever before that I will continue my fitness program, because I have learned how to be flexible. Being flexible has made the whole endeavor feel less oppressive, and I hardly ever miss a session.

Phil's story illustrates the following points:

1. Expanding an exercise program entails the risk that the workout will seem so difficult that you may avoid it altogether.
2. You can still take advantage of periods of especially high

energy and increase your routine. If you are willing to revert to the "basic routine" at the first sign of fatigue or resistance, you will not be endangering the consistency of your workouts.

3. You will carry out your exercise routine most consistently when your routine feels like self-enhancement and not self-oppression. It would be helpful for you to give yourself "standing permission" to end a workout early. You will probably use this permission rarely, as you can usually "get into it" once you have started working out. But permission to end early will lower your resistance to going to the gym on days when you don't initially feel energetic. Therefore, permission to end early will have the net result of fewer missed workouts.

For those readers who have had difficulty maintaining an exercise regimen due to feeling that exercise is and will always be arduous and unpleasant, I hope I have provided some insight and encouragement. You really can change your mind, and therefore your feelings, about exercise if you will keep an open mind.

Types of Exercise

If you were to make fine distinctions, there may be more categories of exercise than I will describe. And, of course, there are areas not discussed here such as speed training and agility training. Nevertheless, without making fine distinctions, I believe it is reasonable to identify six major types of exercise:

- Strength training
- Cardiovascular exercise
- Balance training
- Flexibility training
- Mind-body Integration
- Core Stability training

Chapters four through nine will discuss these six types of exercise.

Chapter 4
Strength training

Strength training is known to reduce the signs
and symptoms of many chronic conditions,
such as back pain, arthritis, heart
disease and diabetes.

Strength training is a type of physical exercise specializing in the use of resistance to induce muscular contraction that builds the strength, endurance, and size of skeletal muscles. Strength training is said to be one of the oldest disciplines. In ancient Greece, Milo of Croton trained for strength by carrying a newborn calf on his back daily. Currently we seldom see anyone carrying animals for strength training. However, it is difficult to miss seeing weight-training equipment in school gymnasiums, commercial fitness centers and sporting goods stores.

There is a wide variety of means to gain knowledge about weight training: books, videos, Internet websites and trainers. I will not endeavor in this volume to provide specific information on the various muscle groups and the exercises used to strengthen them. What I will do is to provide information about the advantages of strength training as well as a number of the concepts and procedures relevant to strength training.

Strength training has many distinct advantages:

1. It has been established that strength training increases bone density. This reduces the risk of osteoporosis, and reduces the risk of fractures, especially as you age.
2. Muscle tissue burns calories more efficiently than does other tissue. Thus, as you gain muscle mass, you may burn more calories and help yourself to control your weight.
3. Muscle strength increases stamina. This will help you to walk long distances, walk up stairs, perform household or outdoor chores, and simply to persist through normal daily activities with less fatigue.
4. Strength training is known to reduce the signs and symptoms of many chronic conditions, such as back pain, arthritis, heart disease and diabetes.
5. There is strong and growing evidence that strength training has considerable mental health benefits, including improved focus and attention, especially for older adults.
6. Strength training provides stamina beyond that required to perform normal daily activities, thus creating a reserve that can maintain our functioning after an illness or injury.

The evidence of mental health benefits of strength training would fill many volumes. A review of this body of work is not considered necessary for this volume. Among others, O'Connor, Herring and Corvalle have reviewed some of the research. They indicate that support for mental health benefits of strength training is impressive. Anxiety, depression, and chronic fatigue can all be reduced, and self-esteem and cognitive functioning can be improved.

There are many popular types of strength training. Four such types are 1. body-weight exercises, 2. machines, 3. lifting fee weights, and 4. resistance tubing. Body weight exercises include very familiar calisthenics such as push-ups and chin-ups. In these exercises, we are using our own body weight as resistance. Some body-weight exercises require only a floor as equipment, and this is one advantage. Machines have the advantage of balancing the weight for you. The machine forces you to make a fixed movement. While this can help build the foundation strength of the major muscle groups, its disadvantage is that it does not require you to use peripheral muscles to stabilize the weights as you lift and release them. Training with free weights does require us to utilize peripheral muscles, and thus may provide better overall strength. Its disadvantage, especially in the early phase of training, could be a somewhat greater chance of muscle strain. Resistance tubing is often used in physical therapy clinics to help rehabilitate injuries such as rotator cuff tears. The rubber tubes are often attached to a fixed structure, such as a doorknob of a closed door, and you can do a variety of exercises by pulling to stretch the tube. You will be introduced to this type of exercise in Chapter 12 on care of the shoulders.

All four types of strength training exercises can help you to build muscle strength. However, if incorrectly performed, they can also cause or aggravate existing injuries to muscles, tendons or ligaments. I strongly advise you to seek guidance before embarking on any but the most basic and gentle program.

How is muscular strength increased?

In his book *Strength Training*, Gareth Jones indicates

> Strength training works by overloading muscles, or groups of muscles, then allowing the muscle tissue to adapt, and then overloading the muscle again. On the cellular level, this works because overloading causes microscopic tears to the muscle cells. The damage is rapidly repaired by your body and the affected muscles regenerate and grow stronger. After you work out, testosterone, insulin-like growth factor, growth hormone, proteins, and other nutrients rush to your muscles to help repair them and make them stronger.

Muscle Strength and Muscle Endurance Training

Muscular strength is defined as the maximum amount of force that a muscle can exert against some form of resistance in a single effort. Muscular endurance is the ability to move your body or an object repeatedly without getting tired. Based on these definitions, lifting a heavy object onto the back of a truck would require muscular strength while shoveling the snow off the length of a driveway would require muscle endurance. For most activities, you use both muscular strength and endurance, though muscular endurance is probably more relevant to the demands you are likely to encounter in your life. For instance, it is not unusual to be asked by a friend or relative to help them with relocating to a new home. You may need to carry dozens of boxes of moderate weight from a truck and into a house or apartment. This task would require predominately muscular endurance.

Muscle Fiber Types

In most fields of knowledge, the more we learn, the more we realize how very complex the world is. And we realize how much more there is that we could learn. This can certainly be said about muscle structure and function. Wayne Westcott gives this overview about muscle fiber types:

> Not all muscle fibers utilize oxygen in the same way. Slow-twitch muscle fibers use oxygen more efficiently and resist fatigue better than fast-twitch fibers. Slow-twitch muscle fibers

are best suited to endurance exercise, while fast-twitch muscle fibers are best suited to brief bouts of strength exercise.

In **Strength Training**, edited by Gareth Jones, slow-twitch and fast-twitch fibers are referred to as "Type 1 fibers" and "Type 2 fibers" respectively. Jones indicates:

> Most of our muscles contain both types of fibers, but some people are genetically gifted with a predominance of Type 2 fibers, giving them a natural aptitude for high intensity, explosive activities, such as weightlifting or sprinting. Others have genetic weighting toward the slow-twitch Type 1 fibers; most long-distance runners and cyclists fall into this category.

Jones goes on to tell us that training can change one type of fiber into another, or alter the way in which fibers work. Thus, we can train ourselves to be more proficient at endurance activities or high intensity, explosive activities by using the appropriate training regimen.

Free Weights and Machines

As previously indicated, weight training can be done with machines or free weights. The advantage of machines is that the weight will remain in a fixed track, with no chance of imbalance. And, you will not have to go to a weight rack, lug the weights over one at a time to a barbell, and set up the barbell in that way.   In addition, lugging weights from a rack to a machine may cause you to put an unbalanced load on your back, which could cause strain or injury. Using machines can help you to develop basic strength.

The disadvantage of machines is that you will not be working the entire sets of muscles. There are portions of the muscles that stabilize what you are lifting, and those muscles are not as engaged with machines. The advantage of free weights is that the stabilizing muscles are in fact engaged, and you get a more complete workout. If you are just now embarking on a weight lifting program, you may want to consider starting with the use of machines until you have built up your foundation strength. After a while, you may want to start substituting some free weight exercises for some of the machines.

Form! Form! Form!
(It is for your body – *not* for the weights!)

Unless you bring a welding torch with you into the gym,
the weights will be the same when you leave
as when you arrived.

Anyone who has ever watched people working out with weights will have witnessed many weight lifters struggling mightily to lift as much weight as they can. They will often attempt this with sudden, jerky or spasmodic movements, and with various body contortions. For instance, someone trying to curl as much weight as he can may jerk the weights upward, bending backward. This is a poor way to isolate the muscle being trained, and is a likely way to become injured. When I see someone working out in this way, I have to fight back the urge to ask him or her some questions: "What are you trying to accomplish? Are you working on your body, or on those weights? Do you not realize that those weights will be unchanged when you leave?"

The point is: ***The important event going on is in your body, not in the weights.*** The amount of weight that goes up and down is irrelevant. Unless you bring a welding torch with you into the gym, the weights will be the same when you leave as when you arrived. It is better to use an amount of weight that you can handle. In that way you can focus on performing the exercise with proper form, engage the targeted muscle group, and train yourself to maintain good posture and balance.

Sets and Reps

When you pick up a free weight, engage a piece of equipment, or do a callisthenic, and perform a movement a number of times, you have performed a "set." The term for each time you perform the movement is a repetition, colloquially termed a "rep." Thus, if you do twenty push-ups, rest a minute and then do twenty more push-ups, you have done two sets of twenty reps each.

In former years, the conventional recommendation in weight lifting was to do three sets of ten repetitions each. The amount of weight was constant. Another typical strategy was "pyramiding," in which at first the weight was increased and reps decreased, then the process was reversed. Thus, five sets were recommended. The table below depicts an hypothetical pyramid method for five sets of bench presses.

Set #	Weight	Repetitions
1	120	10
2	140	8
3	160	6
4	140	8
5	120	10

These and other schemes were developed by "seat-of-the-pants" methods. Athletes and trainers would try out different schemes and would recommend the ones they believed worked best for them. In recent decades, the fields of exercise physiology, exercise biochemistry and biomechanics have changed the older thinking. In 1990 The American College of Sports Medicine recommended one or more sets of resistance exercises for building strength. Many trainers recommend doing one set of an exercise, and performing reps until you cannot complete another rep (known as "failure").

Concentric and Eccentric Phases – and Timing

Assume you are lying on your back on a weight bench with a barbell on a rack above you. Gripping the bar and pushing it up toward the ceiling is the concentric phase of the exercise. Lowering the bar toward your chest is the eccentric phase. Many weight lifters place all their emphasis on the concentric phase, allowing the weight to fall rapidly to the start position. The current thought is that it is best to allow two seconds for the concentric phase and two-to-four seconds for the eccentric.

Breathing

Do not hold your breath during weight training exercises. It is recommended that you breathe continuously throughout the exercise, exhaling during the lifting or pushing phase (concentric) and inhaling during the lowering (eccentric) phase.

A number of the concepts relevant to strength training have been presented. Strength training is an important part of a fitness regimen. You will have improved feelings of vigor and vitality, as well as enhanced self-esteem, when you are the one who can shovel the snow off the driveway, carry the heavy luggage into the airport, and hoist the kayak onto the roof of the car.

There is a variety of means to gain specific knowledge about strength training: books, videos, Internet websites and trainers. Seek information and guidance before embarking on a serious routine. Consider strength training as part of your overall fitness regimen. If at first you find it distasteful and arduous, try at least one time to change your mind about the experience, and to learn to enjoy it. If you continue to experience it as distasteful, drop it. My primary objective is to encourage you to adopt a fitness regimen and to persist with it. You are unlikely to persist with a regimen that you continue to experience as arduous and distasteful. In this book, there are chapters on each of six types of exercise: strength training, aerobic training, balance, flexibility, mind-body integration and core stability. You are unlikely to do them all. Experiment with all six. Drop the types of exercise routines you cannot learn to enjoy. Persist with the types you can enjoy, and you are more likely to develop a regimen with which you can persist for life.

Chapter 5
Aerobic Training

Studies such as the Harvard Health Alumni Study,
published in the Journal of the American Medical
Association in April 1995, report that subjects
who had the highest level of aerobic activity
also had the greatest longevity.

Aerobic exercise (also known as cardiovascular exercise, but now popularly shortened to "cardio") is physical exercise that may be of relatively low, moderate or high intensity, and that depends primarily on calling for the heart and lungs to provide a steady flow of oxygen to adequately meet the energy demands of muscles. Cardiovascular fitness is defined as the ability of your heart, lungs and organs to consume, transport and utilize oxygen. Often, cardio denotes light-to-moderate intensity activities that can be performed for extended periods. The intensity should be between 60 and 80% of maximum heart rate.

The average human heart weights about eleven ounces, beats about 100,000 times per day, and transports 2,000 gallons of blood through 60,000 miles of blood vessels to seventy-five trillion cells. Seventy-two beats per minute is considered to be an average heart rate. However, aerobic training causes the muscles to create new capillaries to meet the increased demand, and the heart becomes more efficient. A typical adult can, with a moderate aerobic workout program, increase heart efficiency so that average heart rate can fall to sixty to sixty-four beats per minute.

Examples of cardiovascular/aerobic exercise are brisk walking, medium to long distance running or jogging, hiking, rowing, kayaking, swimming, and bicycling. In addition, aerobic exercise can be performed on machines such as exercise bikes, stair climbers, treadmills and elliptical training machines. Aerobic exercise became popularized after Air Force physician Kenneth H. Cooper conducted extensive research on over five thousand Air Force Personnel. The idea of sixty percent to eighty percent of maximum heart rate is a legacy of that Air Force research.

Studies such as the Harvard Health Alumni Study, published in the Journal of the American Medical Association in April 1995, report that subjects who had the highest level of aerobic activity also had the highest rate of longevity. In addition, aerobic exercise can be helpful in effecting weight loss. Do not expect miracles in this regard. Keep in mind that it has been calculated that the average person must burn 3500 calories to lose one pound of fat. The good news is that your body is likely to continue to burn more calories for two hours after a 30-minute cardiovascular workout.

Continuous Training

Continuous cardiovascular training is just what it sounds like. It refers to a workout in which a steady pace with steady resistance is maintained throughout the workout. In a fitness center, this exercise might be on a treadmill, a stationary bicycle, a step climber or an elliptical trainer. A thirty-minute cardiovascular workout three-to-five times per week is a typical recommendation.

Many sources recommend, if you are using continuous training, that you exercise at sixty to eighty percent of your maximum rate. One popular definition of "maximum" is derived by subtracting your age from 220. Thus, if you were forty years of age, your maximum training rate would be 220 minus 40, or 180 beats per minute. Let us assume you were aiming for a sixty-to-eighty percent of that figure as a good training rate. If you are forty years of age, you subtract 40 from 220, which gives you a maximum rate of 180. Sixty percent of 180 equals 108 and eighty percent of 180 equals 144. Thus, by that particular formula, 108 to 144 would be considered your training range.

Interval Training

Interval training refers to a workout in which periods of higher intensity training are alternated with periods of a resting pace. "Resting pace" does not denote a period of inactivity, but rather a period in which there is continuous activity, but with the pace and/or resistance reduced. There is no one set program. The following table describes some possibilities.

Intensity Level	Time of exercise	Time of "rest"	Ratio of work/rest
1. Slight increase	10'	4'	5/2
2. Moderate increase	4'	2'	2/1
3. Closer to maximum effort	2.5'	1.5'	5/3
4. As hard as you can go (all out sprint)	30 seconds	2'	1/4

To illustrate, let us assume you will be walking on a treadmill at level 3 – closer to maximum effort. A resting pace might be 3.1 miles per hour at level 4.0 elevation. You might start with two minutes of resting pace. Then, you might raise the speed to 3.8 and the elevation to 7.5 and maintain that pace for 2.5 minutes. Then drop the pace and elevation back to 3.1 and 4.0 respectively for 1.5 minutes. You would then once again do 2.5 minutes at 3.8/7.5, and return to 3.1/4.0 for 1.5 minutes. You could continue until you had completed five intervals of 2.5 minutes each with the higher elevation and pace. Including a final 3-minutes of resting pace, the entire interval workout would have taken 23-24 minutes.

There are several advantages of interval training, including:

- Because of the increased level of effort, you can derive as much benefit from a twenty-to twenty-five minute workout as you would derive from thirty minutes or more of continuous training.
- The changes in intensity, and the attention you must pay to them, may reduce the danger of boredom.
- Outcome studies have demonstrated an improved training rate in the form of increased tolerance for exercise.
- When you are working harder during the training intervals, your motivation to sustain a high effort increases, as you know a resting pace period is coming.

As I will emphasize several times in this book, the workout you do is worth infinitely more than the workout you avoid. The best cardiovascular workout for you is the one you enjoy. If you do not learn to enjoy it, then the best workout for you would be the one you tolerate with the least discomfort.

Chapter 6
Balance Training

Your physical life is not something that takes place for
forty-five minutes in a gym or on a hiking trail.
Every time you move from place to place,
change position or handle objects,
your ability to remain balanced
is engaged.

Balance training is receiving much more attention than in the past. There are now many unusual looking toys seen in gyms, sporting goods stores, and fitness magazines. There are cut-in-half stability balls, small circular "pillow discs", balance wedges and rocker boards. More than just curiosities, they are signs of recognition of the importance balance plays in our safety as well as our fitness.

You may begin balance training in the simplest way. Just stand upright with your feet about two-to-three inches apart, and lift one foot off the floor. Focus your attention on your balance, and hold that position. You will immediately be aware of the adjustments being made by the foot that is on the floor. (As will be mentioned later, the soles of your feet are involved in your body's sense of balance). Set a modest goal to start, such as holding the position of standing on one foot for a count of ten.

If you think back to childhood games and pastimes, you may recall balance exercises among your activities. Perhaps you recall walking on a curbstone to see how many steps you could take without falling off. Or, you may have had a game to see who could hop on one foot for the longest. We did not call it "balance training" then, but that is just what we were doing. We were training ourselves to have improved balance and stability.

Today, competitive athletes recognize that balance training helps them to perform better, and fitness experts know that good balance and a strong core go hand in hand. However, you do not have to be a competitive athlete to add balance training to your fitness regimen. There are many simple exercises you can do at home or at the gym to improve your balance.

You may ask why balance training is so important. Your physical life is not something that takes place for forty-five minutes in a gym or on a hiking trail. Every time you move from pace to place, change position or handle objects, your ability to remain balanced is engaged. Your ability to remain safe from injury (or embarrassment) and to avoid muscle strains may often depend on your balance.

The formal word for the body's method for maintaining balance is "proprioception." It is the body's ability to interpret and use information about your position in space. Proprioception works via a complex array of inputs, including your visual field, your inner ear's perception of gravity, and even tactile input you are receiving from your joints and from the soles of your feet. Based on this input, your body/mind system decides which muscles to adjust to maintain your desired position. It does this when you are standing, walking, or engaging in physical activity. If the inputs become too complex to translate, the system gets overwhelmed and you lose balance. However, just as with other acquired skills, your body/mind system can be trained to function better in this domain.

You are very well acquainted with how people train themselves to have better balance. Watch a toddler who is just getting on his or her feet, and watch the persistent efforts to walk. Recall, if you can, your efforts when you first learned to ride a two-wheel bicycle. Everyone who has ever learned to walk, run, ride a bicycle, skate or ski is very well aware of the process of training our proprioceptive abilities.

You can test your own balance easily. Stand up and prepare to walk forward in a straight line. Place one foot directly in front of the other so that the toes of your back foot touch the heel of your front foot. Keep both feet as flat on the floor as you can. Close your eyes and hold that position. You are doing well if you can maintain your balance for 30 seconds. If you begin swaying or fighting for balance quickly, your balance, at least at that moment in time, could be improved.

If you were to take out a selection of books from the library on balance training, you would be faced with a dizzying array of recommended exercises. A few typically recommended exercises will be included here.

Exercise One – Single leg raise: Stand with your feet together. Take a deep breath and relax, focusing your eyes on a point on the wall in front of you. Lift one foot off the floor and raise your knee. If possible, raise your knee until your thigh is parallel to the floor. Extend your arms out to your sides for extra balance. Hold this position for a set period without letting your raised foot touch the ground, and then repeat on the opposite leg. This exercise will build hip strength as well as enhance your mind-body connection. Your initial challenge is to hold the position and keep still. As you improve that ability, your challenge becomes keeping your knee up for longer periods.

Exercise two – one leg rear lift: Have you ever reached down with your right hand to pick something off the floor, and noticed yourself raising your left leg off the floor behind you as a counterbalance? You were naturally performing a balance exercise. Stand in a natural position and raise your arms to the sides to about shoulder height. Lean slightly forward and, while inhaling, lift one leg to the back. Lead with your heel to engage your buttocks muscles. Lower your leg to the starting position as you exhale. Repeat this motion a comfortable number of times and then switch to the other leg.

This exercise is a core strength exercise called "teaser." It is also a strength and balance exercise. Begin by lying supine. Reach upward with your outstretched hands and your feet until you attain a sense of balance and can hold the position.

Standing on one foot, sweep the other leg back and forth over a stationary object such as an exercise ball.

These are but a few of a multitude of exercises that help with balance and core stability. It is far beyond the purpose of this book to provide more than an introductory idea of this type of training. There are different reasons your balance may a matter of concern to you. You may feel your balance is weak and want to improve it for safety concerns. Alternatively, you may want to acquire extra skill in this area for an athletic purpose. Regardless of your own reason, there are many resources available in libraries, on-line, and through fitness instruction. A number of books are listed in the reference section of this volume.

Chapter 7
Flexibility Training

Stretching helps you to get in touch at a deeper level with
your body's feelings. In a sense, stretching helps you to
know your body. Stretching helps you
understand how your body feels
and what it is capable of while
moving in a variety of ways.

Flexibility or limberness refers to the range of movement in a
joint or joints, as well as the length of muscles that cross the
joints. Flexibility varies very widely between and among
individuals. This is particularly true of differences in the
muscle length of multi-joint muscles. Flexibility in some joints
can be increased to a certain degree by exercise. Stretching
exercises have been a common component of athletic
training for decades, though the theory and techniques have
evolved.

Loss of flexibility can be a predisposing factor for physical
issues such as pain syndromes or balance disorders. It is
widely believed that quality of life is enhanced by improving
and maintaining a good range of motion in the joints.

Individual differences need to be kept in mind as joint function varies from one individual to another.

Flexibility is a pervasive factor in your ability to enjoy being in your body in your daily life. Pay careful attention to how you feel during such common activities as getting in and out of a car, picking an object off the floor, or reaching to place an item on a high shelf. These simple activities can bring you a sense of discomfort or a sense of pleasure, depending on your body's flexibility.

A description of specific stretching exercises for the various muscles and muscle groups throughout the body is beyond the scope of this book. There are many references that can provide you with this information, and you may find some of them listed in the bibliography. This chapter will cover the types of stretching exercises, ideas about why, when and how to stretch, and some information about the physiology of stretching.

Types of Stretches

Depending on your age, gentle reader, you may recall the bouncing toe touches and other jerky, erratic stretching routines from gym class or from the athletic field. These aggressive, bouncing routines are referred to as *ballistic stretching*, and are now out of favor for most purposes. For most purposes, *static stretching* is now in favor as the preferred method for general fitness. Static stretching refers to assuming a challenging but comfortable position and holding it for ten to thirty seconds. Another type of stretching favored by athletes, athletic trainers and physical therapists is **dynamic stretching**. As with static stretching, dynamic stretching involves challenging but comfortable stretches, but entails moving repeatedly, ten to twelve times, though a range of motion. The motions in dynamic stretching are smooth and controlled, in contrast to the jerky, erratic movements of ballistic stretching.

Why Stretch?

In his book entitled **Stretching**, Bob Anderson lists a number of reasons for stretching to be part of your fitness regimen. The benefits he identifies include the following:

- Stretching reduces muscle tension, making the body feel more relaxed.
- Stretching helps coordination by allowing freer and easier movement.
- Stretching helps prevent injuries such as muscle strains, as a flexible, pre-stretched muscle resists stress better than a stiff, un-stretched muscle.
- Stretching helps maintain your current level of flexibility, so that you do not become stiffer as time passes.

In addition, many authors state that stretching helps you to get in touch at a deeper level with your body's feelings. In a sense, stretching helps you to know your body. Stretching helps you understand how your body feels and what it is capable of while moving in a variety of ways. This can lead to better balance, better mind-body integration, and to a better feel for what your body needs and can tolerate when it comes to strength training.

When to Stretch

Stretching may be done anytime, as long as it is not socially inappropriate for the occasion and as long as it does not directly interfere with another activity. The following are among the times when you may decide to stretch:

- After you rise and before you begin your day.
- After sitting or standing in one place for a period of time.
- When you experience the sensation of stiffness.
- Whenever you feel the sensation of nervous tension.
- Before, during and after any vigorous exercise (see discussion that follows).

For many years the conventional practice was to stretch before a sport or activity. It was believed that this would prepare the body for the activity ahead, and would reduce the risk of injury. The disciplines of exercise physiology and exercise biochemistry have in recent years revolutionized this thinking. It has become known that vigorous or extended stretching before a sport or activity may actually increase the risk of injury. The current thought is that *extended stretching* is best done *after* a sport or activity, when the muscles have already become more warm and pliable.

Frederic Delavier is one of many authors who invoke a rubber band analogy. If you stretch a rubber band gently a few times, it will become warmer, but if you stretch it too vigorously, it will break. Extended stretching prior to a sport or activity may reduce muscle elasticity and make the muscle less explosive, thus reducing performance. Thus, warm-up stretching is best done gently. Many activities such as football, baseball, tennis, weight lifting or soccer are fragmented, with moments of high intensity alternating with moments of inactivity. Delavier indicates that stretching during the breaks can have a positive or a negative effect.

> In the best case, stretching allows you to regain muscle tone quickly by enhancing recuperation, which translates to an improvement in performance. In the worst case, stretching can accentuate the loss of muscle tone, which hastens fatigue.

The current thought is that the best time to enhance flexibility via stretching is immediately after a workout. The muscles that were just used are still warm, and this is a good time to enhance flexibility.

How then should we warm up before a sport or activity? Current thinking is that we should use movements that gradually and progressively simulate the activity that will follow. Thus, if you are preparing to play a sport such as basketball or soccer, a good warm-up might include jogging in place, side steps, lifting the knees and hugging them to your chest, small jumps and shoulder rolls.

The Physiology of the Stretch

This is a very complex area. The body has ways of trying to protect itself, and this comes into play when it comes to stretching. First, there is the so-called "stretch reflex," more formally known as the "myotatic reflex." The body's first response to a stretch is to resist the stretch in order to protect against a muscle tear. However, there is a secondary reaction, known as the "Golgi tendon organ reflex," which seeks to reduce the threat of a tear by forcing the muscle to relax. You may even be able to detect these responses as you experiment with stretching exercises.

Some trainers will recommend that you hold a stretch for thirty seconds, believing that the Golgi reflex will enable you to get a deeper stretch. Other trainers will ask you to hold a stretch for 5-15 seconds, release it, and stretch again, believing that the myotatic reflex would otherwise work against an optimal stretch. There seems to be no universally agreed upon method.

My recommendation would be to attempt a given stretch and pay careful attention to what your body is telling you. For instance, suppose you are attempting to stretch your hamstring muscles, as in the following photo.

Move into the stretch position and pay attention. If you feel too much strain, assume that the myotatic reflex is active, and release the stretch. After a 3-5 second break, attempt the stretch again. If the sensation of strain returns, relax again. You may continue in this way, alternating 5-15 seconds stretches with 3-5 second rests. If, on the other hand, you feel the muscle relaxing and allowing an even deeper stretch, you may assume that the Golgi tendon organ reflex is activated, and you may deepen the stretch and hold it for thirty seconds.

Be mindful of the procedure that feels most comfortable for you. The procedure with which you are comfortable is the one you are most likely to make part of your routine. As I will write repeatedly throughout this volume, the best regimen for you is the one with which you are comfortable, and that you therefore do not dread.

Chapter 8
Mind-body Integration

For our purposes here, we are looking at the term
"mind body integration" in a generic sense,
to denote any activity in which you are
fully present and aware of what
your body is doing.

As the name indicates, mind-body training refers to techniques that emphasize simultaneous awareness of mind and body to achieve a desired result. This covers a very wide variety of methods and domains, including yoga, martial arts, Tai Chi, meditation, mindfulness training, dance, acting and some forms of psychotherapy.

The idea that body and mind are separate entities is primarily a western idea, which has been traced back to the 17th century French philosopher Rene Descartes. His idea was called "mind-body dualism," and he argued that the nature of the mind is completely different from that of the body. Eastern practices such as yoga, Tai Chi and martial art forms have for millennia emphasized integration of mind and body, but this idea caught on later in western thought. The physiologist Edmund Jacobson, who worked at Harvard, Cornell and Bell Laboratories, devised a method called "progressive relaxation," which is part of the stock and trade of your author. Herbert Benson was another western pioneer of the idea that the mind and body are one system, and he emphasized reducing stress responses through the relaxation response.

For our purposes here, we are looking at the term "mind body integration" in a generic sense, to denote any activity in which you are fully present and aware (the current popular term is "mindful") of what your body is doing. This has the benefit of increased present-centered focus, which can clear the mind of distracting or extraneous thoughts or images. You may then perform a physical exercise, or other activity, with better focus and control. This will aid you in attaining better balance, and to perform in a more precise and efficient manner.

Finally – A Blending of Eastern and Western Traditions

It may well be that civilization will benefit far more from a
blending of eastern and western traditions
than by their remaining apart.

Before describing Tai Chi and Yoga, I want to diverge a bit. When I studied ancient history in high school, there was a recurrent theme. When the Greeks turned back the Persians after the famous battles of Thermopylae, Salamis and

Plataea, my history book stated that had the Persians defeated the Greeks, western culture would have been inundated with eastern ideas, but that the victorious Greeks "saved the West for better things." Later, after the titanic struggles between the Romans and the Carthaginians ended with a Roman victory, the history book stated that if the Carthaginians had defeated the Romans, western culture would have been inundated with eastern ideas, but that the victorious Romans "saved the West for better things." I accepted what the book said at face value. It was not until about eight or nine years later that I had different thoughts.

It occurred to me that the strength of the West has been our ability to develop physical sciences and technology. The West has been very much outwardly directed. The strength of the eastern traditions has been the ability to develop mind/body techniques. The East has been more inwardly directed. Each tradition has its strengths and its liabilities. It may well be that civilization will benefit far more from a blending of these traditions than by their remaining apart. The emergence in the West of Tai Chi and Yoga, as well as acupuncture, acupressure and other methods, is a manifestation of an integration of eastern and western ideas.

A Brief Description of Tai Chi

There are many accounts and legends about the origins of Tai Chi. Since it was reportedly taught in the strictest secrecy, its origins may be lost in antiquity. Tai Chi is believed, by some practitioners of the art, to have been brought to China in the fifth century A.D. by a wandering Buddhist monk. Tai Chi can be described in a number of ways. I have heard it described as the study of circular motion. If you have ever watched Tai Chi forms being practiced, or have had Tai Chi instruction yourself, you know that the movements are smooth and circular, in contrast to the abrupt and linear movements of systems such as Tae Kwon Do. Tai Chi can be simply described as meditation through movement. And, significantly, it can be described as the art of cultivating and utilizing "Chi," or life force. Through a combination of the form, focused breathing and meditation, the practitioner seeks to store Chi in a place just below the abdomen. If you had ever seen a Tai Chi master using what seems to be little or no physical effort to match the power of bigger, harder-working martial artists, you would not doubt that, in some way, energy can be stored and called upon through this discipline. Tai Chi Chuan, which can be translated as "perfect boxing," is the martial arts aspect of Tai Chi. But the methods are very often used as a meditation-through-movement without a combat orientation.

If you have no interest in using Tai Chi for defense, it is a delightful method of achieving balance and mind-body integration by learning elegant, enjoyable forms. Moreover, you may be able to bring the general sense and awareness of your Tai Chi practice to other, more mundane tasks in your life, and find yourself performing activities in a smoother, more elegant manner. The study of Tai Chi typically begins with learning a form, which is very much like learning a series of dance steps. These dance steps are flowing and involve circular movements. All movement originates from your abdomen. In a Tai Chi form, you would never be leaning out with your upper body.

In her book *The Everything Tai Chi and QiGong Book*, Ellae Elinwood describes Tai Chi as follows:

> Tai Chi is a series of positions, one flowing into the next. By gently twisting and turning as you balance and re-balance your arms and legs into a lovely, unhurried, steady, graceful sequence, every portion of the body is used, refreshed and revitalized.

The following three pictures, showing poses from a Five Element Form adapted from Tai Chi Sun style, illustrate that Tai Chi may be used as a gentle, non-martial method to enhance mind-body integration.

Fair Lady Works the shuttle

Single Whip

Play Guitar

Notes on the Development of Taoism, Traditional Chinese Medicine, Qigong and Tai Chi

If you do any reading about the origins and development of these philosophies and disciplines, you will find some differing accounts. Therefore, please accept the following account as an approximation.

Taoism is the original religion of China, and its roots go back over five thousand years. Taoism is known for its emphasis on nature, harmony, balance, chi energy and mysticism. Taoist practice and ethics vary depending on the particular school, but in general emphasize the concept of action through non-action. Some central Taoist principles are "naturalness", simplicity, spontaneity, and the Three Treasures: compassion, moderation, and humility.

A central tenet of Chinese philosophy is that of the forces of yin and yang. Many tangible dualities, such as female and male, light and dark, and water and fire, are thought of as physical manifestations of the duality of yin and yang. These are conceptualized as complementary, rather than contrary forces, giving rise to one another and helping to create the fabric of the natural world. The principle of yin and yang implies that the whole is greater than the assembled parts. Everything is believed to have both yin and yang aspects. For instance, shadow cannot exist without light. Either of the two major aspects may be more strongly present in a particular object, person, activity, food, et cetera.

The duality of yin and yang is central to many branches of classical Chinese science and philosophy. For instance, it is a primary guiding principle of traditional Chinese medicine, and a central principle of different forms of Chinese martial arts and exercise, including QiGong (pronounced Chee Kung) and Tai Chi.

The Force is an energy field, generated by all living things.
It surrounds us, and penetrates us.
It binds the galaxy together.

- Obewan Kenobi
(*Star Wars, A New Hope*)

Producer George Lucas was undoubtedly influenced by the concept of chi and by Tai Chi masters when he conceived of the idea of "The Force" and of Jedi Knights in his Star Wars movies. In Chinese tradition, chi is a vital resource, normally circulating within us, which we can use for self-enhancement and healing.

You will find differing accounts of the distinction between QiGong and Tai Chi. QiGong is typically described as the study of the breath, with an emphasis on an awareness of breath as the source of life and energy. Tai Chi is the art of the cultivation and mastery of chi (life energy). Chi is stored in the body and the practitioner learns to call on chi by the practice of forms and breathing. (Do not expect to find unanimity about this distinction if you do further reading).

Yoga

Just as does Tai Chi, Yoga teaches mind-body integration and balance. Yoga is also known for its emphasis on flexibility. Yoga is an ancient art and science that originated in India. In Sanskrit, "Yoga" means "union." Developed as a system to strengthen and align the body, to quiet and focus the mind, and to prepare for meditation, the practice of yoga attempts to join body, mind and spirit into an integrated whole.

Yoga is an integral part of the Buddhist tradition. For those who practice Buddhism, it is a way to fully feel as though you are one with the Buddha and all entities in the Universe. That being said, one does not need to adhere to these beliefs in order to practice yoga. However, some adherents practice it as a spiritual pathway, and most of its practitioners do adhere to certain rituals. In addition, Yoga does involve a code of ethics toward yourself and others. Though practiced in the East for thousands of years, Yoga had few proponents in the West prior to the twentieth century.

There are actually at least five types of yoga. In the West, we typically practice *Hatha* yoga, which usually focuses on the physicality of the forms, or *asanas*. By practicing the poses, practitioners of Hatha Yoga can enhance flexibility and balance, tone the body, and build stamina. Hatha Yoga is actually a form of what is known as Raja Yoga. This is the yoga of science, and its focus is to use meditation as a means to control and purify the mind, to unify inner and outer truths and achieve union with the Universe.

Studying yoga does not mean being perpetually blissful. Rather, through the poses, breathing, and mind/body integration, we may become better able, successfully and peacefully, to navigate the world of people, events, responsibilities and emotions.

There are many yoga forms and poses, and many variations of each depending on the particular school of yoga as well as on the style of the instructor. Poses vary from gentle and easy to energetic and demanding.

If you should read about yoga, you will be faced with a vast array of information about such topics as proper body alignment, improving the emotions and the spirit, and mythological stories. Methods and interpretations vary greatly from school to school, and from instructor to instructor.

The Warrior Poses

I have teased out what I hope is helpful information about three Warrior poses. I have chosen the Warrior poses for two reasons. First, they are among the most iconic postures in yoga. Secondly, they are enjoyable to perform.

Many of the eastern mind/body arts include the concept of "the spiritual warrior." In yoga, the warrior poses represent a story of battle described in the Bhagavad Gita. The warrior poses are a re-enactment of the stances of a warrior under the command of Shiva. Students are often encouraged to embody the spirit of the warrior as they assume these formidable postures.

The warrior poses are not among the most difficult yoga poses to perform. In terms of difficulty, I rate them about a "five on a ten-scale" of difficulty. Nevertheless, they are strong stances that provide a counterpart to some of the more sedate and contemplative aspects of yoga practice. Although the warrior poses help develop physical strength, they are perhaps even more an expression of the inner battle the mind and heart must fight to overcome the inner demon of self-ignorance. They challenge us to develop strength, focus and confidence.

Warrior One is essentially a strong lunge, with your front knee bent and your back leg straight. Your hips and chest face forward. Regular practice of Warrior One increases flexibility in the hips and strengthens and tones the legs, ankles and feet. In addition, this powerful stance may enhance inner strength and courage, allowing you to open up to yourself and others.

Warrior Two requires strength and stability as well as flexibility in the hips and upper body. It emphasizes a key principle of yoga poses: the balance of steadiness and ease.

Exalted Warrior is a pose embodying a sense of triumph and of opening up to the world. It may release tension in the intercostal muscles around the ribs and allow freer, deeper breathing.

Warrior One

In the Warrior One pose, the practitioner strides forward into a strong lunge, with arms stretched upward, fingers pointing to the sky. Although the stride is wide, weight is evenly balanced on the two feet. The pose represents, in the Bhagavad Gita, the warrior emerging from the Earth.

Warrior Two

Also a strong lunge, in Warrior Two there is a stretching, or sense of elongation, from fingertips to fingertips as the arms are extended strongly forward and behind. This pose represents, in the Bhagavad Gita, the warrior locating his foe.

Exalted Warrior

In Exalted Warrior, the back hand rests on the leg above the knee. The feeling of the pose is strong and triumphant. This pose represents, in the Bhagavad Gita, the warrior's triumph.

A note about yoga poses

We are not all built the same, and this applies to our tendons and ligaments, and to the ways in which our bodies can stretch and flex. There is a classic yoga pose called the "lotus position," in which the person sits, with knees bent and with each foot resting on the opposite knee. Attaining this pose, or any other pose requiring significant stretching and flexing, is *not* the goal of yoga. If you should find yourself in a yoga class in which the instructor tries to push and bend your limbs into a position that is unnatural for you, seek a different class with a different instructor.

Diaphragmatic Breathing

Breathing is an integral part of mind-body methods such as yoga and Tai Chi. Oftentimes, individuals will breathe inefficiently without even knowing it. They may develop a breathing habit that prevents them from filling their lungs adequately with air. As they inhale, they will suck in their stomachs and expand their chests. While this may be an impressive pose for pictures, it is not a healthy a way of giving your lungs access to as much oxygen as your body needs. Try placing your hand on your abdomen as you breathe in, slowly and evenly, through your nose. Pay attention to your abdomen, and the hand you have placed on it. Practice allowing your abdomen to rise, which is caused by the expansion of your lungs as your diaphragm descends.

The inner peace of Yoga and the smooth, elegant,
well-coordinated motion of Tai Chi
can potentially become part
of all your activities.

You have been introduced to Tai Chi and Yoga, two significant methods to attain mind-body integration. Please remember that mind-body integration is not confined to the time in which you are engaged in a form or pose. An object of these disciplines is to enable the practitioner to cultivate a way of being that can pervade all the activities of your life. The inner peace of Yoga and the smooth, elegant, well-coordinated motion of Tai Chi can potentially become part of all your activities. This practice can enable you to more comfortably and efficiently shift your attention between and among tasks and obligations. It can help you to be more patient and understanding in interpersonal interactions. It can help you respond more effectively to your body's needs when engaging in other fitness routines. In addition, it can help you to become more relaxed, peaceful and happy in your life.

Chapter 9
Core Stability Training

Your core is the common link between your lower body, where forces are generated, and your upper body, where forces are applied by the upper limbs.

Core stability training is a type of strength training and has gained wide acceptance in the past decade or so. The core of your body is the area surrounding your trunk, where there are said to be twenty-nine muscles in your lower back, abdomen, hips and pelvis. Dahm and Smith describe your core as "the common link between your lower body, where forces are generated, and your upper body, where forces are applied by the upper limbs." Your core muscles act as stabilizers for the rest of your body.

Take a moment to imagine lifting a heavy suitcase. If you did not engage the muscles in your core, you would fall over as soon as you tried to lift. You can imagine your core serving as that stabilizing common link if you take a few moments to imagine lifting an item down from a high shelf, opening up a heavy door, raking leaves, shoveling snow (for persons in snow territory), throwing a ball, hitting a tennis shot, or paddling a canoe or kayak. Now, when you are actually engaged these activities, pay attention to what your body feels like, and you will get a clear idea of what the phrase "engaging your core" means.

The Origins of Core Stability Training

There are now a number of core stability training systems. I will discuss Pilates, as this appears to have been a prime mover for this branch of the fitness movement. Joseph H. Pilates was born in 1883 in Germany. Pilates was a sickly child and suffered from asthma, rickets, and rheumatic fever; and he dedicated his entire life to improving his physical strength. He studied bodybuilding, yoga, Kung Fu and gymnastics. Pilates came to believe that the "modern" life-style, bad posture, and inefficient breathing lay at the roots of poor health. He ultimately devised a series of exercises and training-techniques and engineered all the equipment, specifications, and tuning required to teach his methods properly.

He moved to England in 1912, and earned a living as a professional boxer, circus-performer, and self-defense trainer at police schools and Scotland Yard. Nevertheless, the British authorities interned him during World War I along with other German citizens. While confined, he taught wrestling and self-defense, and began refining and teaching his minimal equipment system of mat exercises that later became "Contrology."

In about 1925, Pilates emigrated from Britain to the United States. On the ship to America, he met his future wife Clara.

The couple founded a studio in New York City and directly taught and supervised their students well into the 1960s. Their method - "Contrology" - encourages the use of the mind to control muscles. It focuses attention on core postural muscles that help keep the body balanced and provide support for the spine. In particular, Pilates exercises teach awareness of breath and of alignment of the spine, and strengthen the deep torso and abdominal muscles.

Pilates methods teach control of the movement of the body by creating flow through the use of appropriate transitions. Once precision has been achieved, the exercises are intended to flow within and into each other in order to build strength and stamina. In other words, the Pilates technique helps you become strong with the ability to move freely.

When practitioners exhale, they are instructed to note the engagement of their deep abdominal and pelvic floor muscles, and to maintain this engagement as they inhale. Essentially, Pilates began what is now widely accepted as an important part of training for many athletes: core stability training.

Through the techniques of Joseph Pilates, athletes and dancers nowadays have an advantage of being stronger than ever before.

Joseph Pilates wrote several books, including **Return to Life through Contrology** and **Your Health**. He was also a prolific inventor, with over 26 patents.   Joe and Clara had a number of disciples who continued to teach variations of his method. In some cases they focus exclusively on preserving the method, and the instructor-training techniques they had learned, during their studies with Joe and Clara.

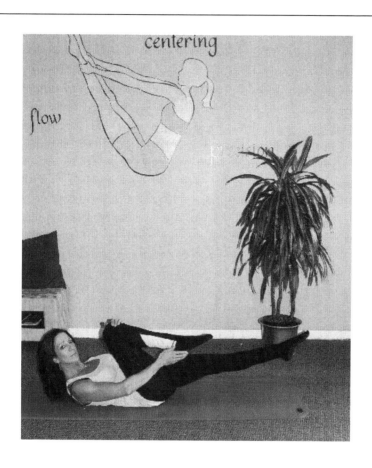

Single Leg Stretch. Focus - abdominals, coordination and stabilization. The focus of the exercise is the abdominal muscles, as well as coordination and stability of the trunk.

Mermaid. Focus - intercostal muscles (breathing muscles) and back extensors. In this exercise, the practitioner lengthens the intercostal muscles and the extensors.

"Eve's Lunge" on the Reformer. The focus is on the hip extensors and gluteal muscles

Chest Expansion on Trapeze. The focus is on strengthening the shoulder girdle, as well as trunk stabilization

Chapter 10
Refuel and Recover after Exercise

Use your best knowledge of nutrition, augment it
with new information from reliable sources,
and maintain good nutritional habits
a reasonable amount of the time.

The body's fuel is glycogen, which consists of long chains of glucose molecules that are stored in the liver, muscles and brain cells. During exercise, the body uses glycogen as fuel, and uses fat as necessary. An intense exercise session can leave the body's fuel stores depleted.

In order to meet future demands, it is important that we refuel our body's energy stores. Failure to recover sufficiently will result in fatigue, which has been defined as an activity-induced loss of ability to exert or maintain overall effort and muscular force. Fatigue can lead to muscle soreness, impaired sleep efficiency, reduced appetite, gastrointestinal distress, and an overall drop in performance. It can even lead to reduced effectiveness of the body's immune system.

The issue of refueling the body after exercise has been an area of debate in the past. Operators of stores that sell sports nutrition products have been telling us for years that we need an influx of protein soon after a workout. There now seems to be growing evidence that they have been correct. However, an even more important post-workout need is to replenish the body's glycogen stores with carbohydrates. Greg Cox, senior sports dietitian, states, "Failure to consume carbohydrate in the immediate phase of post-exercise recovery leads to very low rates of glycogen restoration."

Some sources believe that refueling after a workout is a two-stage process, including an immediate phase, within thirty minutes of exercise completion, and a meal approximately two hours later. Interestingly, some sources state that the types of carbohydrates consumed should differ in stages one and two.

What Is the Glycemic Index?

The glycemic index is a number denoting the speed with which your body converts the carbohydrates in a food into glucose. Foods with a high glycemic index cause our blood sugar to shoot up rapidly.

The lower the glycemic index, the less impact the food has on your blood sugar:

- 55 or less: Low (good)
- 56- 69:   Medium
- 70 or higher: High (bad)

For general health purposes, it is usually recommended that we limit our intake of high glycemic index foods. However, there is a school of thought that, during the first thirty minutes after exercise, high glycemic index foods are beneficial for the restoration of glycogen supplies. In addition, an influx of easily assimilated protein, such as egg whites or a protein shake is recommended.

The next pages will contain charts of twelve high glycemic index foods and twelve low glycemic index foods according to the February 2015 Harvard Medical School's Health Publication.

High Glycemic Index Foods

Type of Food	Glycemic Index	Serving Size	Glycemic load per serving
Baked russet potato	111	150 g	33
Fruit roll-ups	99	30 g	24
Corn flakes	93	30 g	23
White rice	89	150 g	43
Instant mashed potatoes	87	150 g	17
Instant oatmeal	83	250 g	30
Pretzels, oven baked	83	30 g	16
Rice cakes	82	25 g	17

Waffles	76	35 g	10
Graham crackers	74	25 g	14
Instant cream of wheat	74	250 g	17
White bread	71	30 g	10

Low Glycemic Index Foods

Type of Food	Glycemic Index	Serving Size	Glycemic load per serving
100% whole grain bread	51	30 g	7
Brown rice	50	150 g	16
Spaghetti, white, boiled	46	180 g	22
Apple	39	120 g	6
Ice cream, premium	38	50 g	3
Canned tomato juice	38	250 ml	4
Carrots, average	35	80 g	2
Skim milk	32	250 ml	4
Salted cashews	27	50 g	3
Grapefruit	25	120 g	3
Chick peas, average	10	150 g	3
Hummus	6	30 g	0

Although high glycemic foods are recommended by some sources within thirty minutes of a workout, the recommended meal approximately two hours after exercise calls for lean protein, nuts and low glycemic carbohydrates.

The measures you take to refuel your body's glycogen and protein stores will, of course, depend on a number of factors:

- Your goals for exercise (e.g. competition, high fitness, moderate fitness, maintenance of general health).
- Your home, work and mealtime schedule.
- The timing of your next physical exertion, et cetera.

Your fitness will depend not only on exercise, but also on good nutrition, sleep and a strong mental attitude. Use your best knowledge of nutrition, augment it with new knowledge from reliable sources, and maintain good nutritional habits a reasonable amount of the time.

Chapter 11
Care of Your Back

The first back exercise is simply to lie on your back, with your knees bent, focusing your attention on keeping your back flat on the floor. As shown in the picture below, you should not be able to slide a ruler under the small of your back.

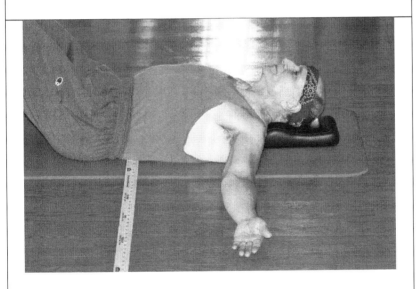

The next exercise is to pull your knees up to your chest, all the time focusing your attention on keeping your back flat on the floor.

Next, continue lying on your back with your back flat against the floor. Pull one foot back so it is flat on the floor close to your buttocks. Raise the other leg in a smooth motion, continuing to focus on your back remaining flat on the floor.

precision

A gentle twisting and stretching exercise for the hips and lower back will help you remain comfortable and may help prevent strains. This stretch will give flexibility to the quadratus lumborum muscles near the sides of your lower back. Lie on your back with your knees bent and your heels near your buttocks. Cross one foot over and place it on the floor against the opposite knee. Placing your arms to the side to isolate the lower back and hips, gently roll to the side, as pictured below. Hold the stretch as long as it is comfortable, up to thirty seconds, and then repeat on the other side.

This is a back strengthening exercise. Start on your hands and knees. Lift and straighten your right leg behind you and straighten your left arm in front of you. Alternate from side to side. Do the exercise slowly, and perform the number of repetitions with which you are comfortable.

You would do well to begin your day with a flexible spine. One way to limber up your spine is to alternate between two Yoga poses known as "cat" and "cow," pictured below.

"CAT"

"COW"

Another way to continue to begin your day with an active, flexible spine would be to alternate between two Yoga poses known as "cobra" and "child pose," pictured below.

"COBRA"

"CHILD POSE"

It is in your best interest to pay careful attention to maintaining the strength and flexibility of your back. Your back in involved in virtually every movement of your body, and even a relatively minor strain or sprain can limit your mobility and cause you to feel debilitated. If you have or have had any significant problems in this area, please consult an orthopedist or an osteopathic physician and then a physical therapist. Use the advice of those professionals to design an appropriate exercise regimen for you.

Chapter 12
Care of Your Shoulders

How many times have you heard someone say they had a rotator cuff problem? The probable answer is many times. In fact, when I looked up "rotator cuff" on the Internet, this is the first definition I encountered:

> "a capsule with fused tendons that supports the arm at the shoulder joint ***and is often subject to injury***"

There are four muscles in the rotator cuff:
- Teres minor
- Infraspinatus
- Supraspinatus
- Subscapularis

As important as these muscles are for the stability of the shoulder, they are not large, strong muscles. They therefore are subject to tearing. One very frequent cause of a rotator cuff tear is reaching for something, such as a car door, for stability to try to prevent a fall. Individuals may also injure their rotator cuffs while handling a heavy suitcase, or performing sports or jobs with repeated overhead motion.

Since the rotator cuff muscles are small and subject to injury, it is very advantageous to exercise them to optimize their strength. If you believe you have an injured rotator cuff, consult an orthopedist or osteopath, as well as a physical therapist, before embarking on a program of rehabilitation. If you have no injury or discomfort in the area, there is in all likelihood no danger in starting to exercise this area on your own. Rotator cuff exercises may be done with an elastic band of the type found in physical therapy facilities, or small dumbbells.

The Internal Rotation

Wrap or loop one end of your exercise elastic around a doorknob or a heavy piece of equipment (anchor). Stand with your feet about shoulder width apart and grasp the elastic. Your distance from your anchor will determine how strenuous this exercise will be. Start with your elbow close to your side and your arm to the side. With a smooth, steady motion, pull your fist in to the midline of your body, keeping your elbow tucked in close to your side. Adjust your distance from the anchor so that ten or twelve repetitions will tire you.

The External Rotation

This is essentially the reverse of the internal rotation. It may feel more awkward, and it may feel like more of a challenge to keep your elbow close to your side. In the picture above, the elastic is being pulled to the individual's right, and toward the left of the page.

Shoulder Flexion

As previously indicated, the muscles of the rotator cuff are not large and strong. You will be using much smaller weights for these exercises than you would for many other strength-building exercises. For the shoulder flexion strengthening exercise, stand straight with your feet close together. Begin by holding dumbbells in each hand at your side. You will be maintaining a dual focus. You will focus on your core as you stabilize your body for the lift, and on a smooth motion as, keeping your arm straight, you raise the dumbbell to eye level in a smooth motion. Keep the dumbbell in a horizontal position so that you are lifting the back or your hand toward the ceiling. Use dumbbells of a weight that allows you to perform 12 to 15 repetitions without undue strain. Maintaining good form is more important than using more weight.

Shoulder Abduction

As previously indicated, the muscles of the rotator cuff are not large and strong. You will be using much smaller weights for these exercises than you would for many other strength-building exercises. For the shoulder abduction strengthening exercise, you will stand with your feet apart about shoulder width. Unlike the shoulder flexion exercise, you will be holding the dumbbells in a vertical position, rather than a horizontal, position. You will neither raise the dumbbells directly in front of you, nor at your side. Raise the dumbbells in between those points, at about forty-five degrees from center.

The picture below could give the impression of action outward to the sides, but that is not the case. Raise the dumbbells from your side in an upward motion at a forty-five degree angle from center. As with the shoulder flexion exercise, you will be maintaining a dual focus. You will focus on your core as you stabilize your body for the lift, and on a smooth motion as, keeping your arm somewhat straight, you raise the dumbbell to shoulder level in a smooth motion.

The Baseball Throw

Fasten one end of the elastic to an anchor, such as a doorknob. Begin this exercise very carefully to ensure you will not strain your arm or shoulder. Begin by standing at a distance from the anchor such that the elastic is taut, but with no tension. Grasp your end of the elastic and think of it as a ball to be thrown. Focus on your balance as you go through a throwing motion. Experiment with a few throws to be sure you are experiencing a comfortable amount of tension. Then perform twenty to thirty repetitions, focusing all the time on maintaining balance.

You may want to have some fun with this. You could use it as a balance and core exercise as well. As shown on the next pictures, you could imagine, for instance, that you are a baseball pitcher.

He goes into his wind-up . . .

... A N D ...

He delivers

A Few Notes

- Prevention is preferable to cure. It is better for shoulder strengthening to be part of your normal exercise routine, and to avoid injury, than to have to rehabilitate an injury.
- If you have experienced what you believe is an injury to this area, seek medical attention immediately. An injury may be a mild strain and inflammation of a muscle or tendon leading to no permanent damage. However, it could also be a partial or complete tear of a muscle. Partial tears typically require rest followed by rehabilitation exercises to strengthen the undamaged portion of the muscle. Extensive or complete tears may require surgery for repair. If surgery is needed, time is of the essence to maximize success. In any event, seek medical attention immediately to be sure.

*** Note from Author ***

The following two chapters have been contributed by Chris Crawford, a fitness instructor at Pima Community College in Tucson, Arizona. She has both personal and professional experiences that have led to a unique and important perspective on the subject of personal fitness.

Chapter 13
A Personal Journey

By Chris Crawford

I want to advance the idea that physical fitness
can play a role in many aspects of
our lives and our health.

I want to share with our readers a very intense and personal journey that took me from health to cancer and back to health. Years ago, I was diagnosed with cancer. My oncologist told me I would have to take a leave of absence from work during the course of chemotherapy. He told me authoritatively that he would be recommending this even if I had a sedentary job. Of course, as a fitness instructor and personal trainer, my job was anything but sedentary. He suggested that I file for disability benefits and forget about work for an extended period of time.

My personal conviction was I would be better off continuing to work. Fitness was an integral part of my life, and contributed to my feelings of strength, health and self-esteem. It did not seem right for me to give up a source of my strength. Yet here was my physician telling me otherwise. In our society, we tend to hold a physician's opinion as sacrosanct. We have all heard persons explain something they were doing by stating, "Doctor's orders!" So here I was, between my own conviction and my doctor's orders.

First, I believed that my immune system depended to an extent on my emotional well-being. Secondly, my emotional well-being depended on my getting up in the morning with what Dr. Mike Slavit calls his mantra: "a place to be, people to see and a function to perform." Third, there was mutualism between my students and myself. They needed me and I needed them. I felt my emotional well-being depended to at least some extent on not letting my students down. Fourth, I had been preaching the virtues of exercise and fitness for so long that I felt an obligation to set an example. I felt I had to live up to the ideals I had supported. Eventually, I decided to go against my doctor's orders and with my own convictions. Doing so gave me a sense of purpose; it gave me a reason to keep going every day, even when it was a struggle to do so.

I ended up having a mastectomy. After the surgery, I awakened in recovery next to a 24-year old woman who had had the same surgery. We were then assigned to the same room on the hospital floor. My roommate eventually had to have a catheter because she was not strong enough to sit up on her own, much less get out of bed. I was able to get up immediately without a problem. I attributed this to having maintained my body strength with years of exercise.

The day after my surgery, the doctors and nurses did not want to release me until I proved that I could tolerate the pain medication they wanted me to take. I informed them that I was not in pain and did not require medication. The nurses told me that once the morphine wore off I would not be able "to get on top of the pain" if I did not immediately start taking the medication. I asked them when I had received the last morphine shot, and they said 3:00 a.m. I asked them how long the morphine lasted, and was told about four hours. I informed them that as it was 9:00 a.m., I had been without morphine for six hours, and I would not be taking any pain pills. My prediction was correct.

Since then, I have had several reconstructive surgeries, and have still taken no post-surgery pain pills. Nurses tell stories about me, having found it unusual that I was able to wake up after surgery happy, comfortable and ready to go home. I believe my body has been resilient because I have worked on physical fitness for so long. I am not writing this to discourage anyone else from taking medication to alleviate pain and discomfort. That is a personal choice and *I would not want our readers to compare their choices with mine.* I do want to advance the idea that physical fitness plays a role in many aspects of our lives, our health and our resilience.

Chapter 14
The Power of Exercise to Transform Lives
By Chris Crawford

*Physical exercise and fitness are far too often overlooked
as potential responses to problems in the areas
of physical health and mental health.*

As western civilization has evolved, our attitudes and practices regarding health and health maintenance have gone in a particular direction. We have a marked tendency to look outside ourselves rather than within ourselves for answers to and remedies for health related issues. Consider the issue of high blood pressure. Physicians are quick to prescribe medicines to attempt to remedy this condition, rather than to encourage patients to change habits in the areas of exercise, nutrition and physical relaxation. Similarly, we seek relief from headaches through pain relieving medicines far more often than we reduce our state of arousal through relaxation or meditation.

Physical exercise and fitness are far too often overlooked as potential, effective responses to problems in the areas of physical health and mental health. The following anecdote is an account of an actual individual whose life condition improved in the context of exercise classes.

David was a man in his sixties who had had a heart attack a year before meeting me. His physician had advised him to lose fifty pounds. Almost all of us are aware of how difficult a proposition weight loss can be. We live in a culture in which we are continually bombarded – on billboards, television advertising and elsewhere – with the message that "food is fun." Many persons grow up in homes in which food is used as a means of giving comfort. Food is very frequently a central feature of social and recreational activities. Our equating food with emotional comfort can follow us throughout our lives. Reducing food intake can therefore feel like a significant social, emotional and recreational deprivation.

David was very discouraged about his prospects to conform to his physician's order and to lose weight. He decided to join an exercise class, and enrolled in the author's class. David participated with modest effort and enthusiasm at first, but he did continue to participate. At first, his weight loss was very slow. It took him about six weeks to lose his first two pounds. Good things were happening nonetheless. Due to his recent heart attack, he was seeing his doctor frequently. When he had first begun his exercise classes, he had been on a plethora of medications totaling twenty-five pills per day. Despite only having lost two pounds, his vital signs and laboratory results had improved, almost certainly due to the exercise regimen. This convinced his doctor to reduce his medication, and he was down from twenty-five to fifteen pills per day.

The medication reduction was a very encouraging sign to David, and it greatly increased his motivation, both to exercise more intensely and to be more careful about his diet. David's account may be instructive.

> After my heart attack, I was very discouraged. I saw my health condition as something totally outside my control. I knew the doctor wanted me to lose weight, but I really struggled. I felt guilty about eating, and then the guilt caused me to soothe myself with more food. It was a vicious cycle, and I felt helpless.
>
> When I started attending exercise class, I exercised dutifully, but without real enthusiasm. My efforts to control overeating were sporadic at best. But after about three weeks of regular exercise, I began to feel differently. I felt stronger and more vigorous. When my doctor told me my blood pressure and cholesterol numbers had improved, I really started to become encouraged. My enthusiasm and effort in exercise class shot up. I really felt that my efforts had an effect, so I no longer felt helpless. It all started with exercise class, and I am feeling better and

better about the physical activity. At first, it had felt like drudgery, but I am actually looking forward to the physical activity, and am enjoying it. Most of all, I no longer feel that my health condition is something outside my control.

David's situation illustrates a few important concepts. Perhaps the most important is the idea advanced in chapter three: individuals who may at first experience exercise as drudgery can learn to enjoy the activity. A second important point is that even if exercise does not immediately result in weight loss, it can give the person a feeling of increased vigor and strength. And third, the medical functioning of the body can be positively influenced by exercise.

Chapter 15
Can't I Just Make it Fun?

There is nothing in and of itself about exercise
that is unpleasant or arduous. You can
learn to love exercise.

Many people are resistant to exercise for the sake of exercise. They make comments such as, "I don't mind exercise if I can kid myself into it by having fun." They exercise if they can play volleyball or some other activity in which the purpose is "fun-and-games," and in which exercise is a byproduct, but not the purpose, of the activity. Essentially, they feel they must distract themselves from the fact that they are exercising. Another typical pattern is for people to insist on having an exercise partner. Therefore, if they go for brisk walks or go to a gym, they do it with a partner and distract themselves, with conversation, from the fact of exercise.

My position on these two methods of motivation is that it is better to exercise through fun and games or by use of a companion than to not exercise at all. However, I believe quite strongly that exercise programs based either on fun-and-games or on companionship are vulnerable to failure. There may be no fun activity available due to a number of factors, and an exercise companion may often be unavailable as well. I have seen dozens of persons give up their exercise program because their exercise partner lost interest, moved away, discontinued their gym membership or had a schedule change that precluded the gym or the hiking trail. If you really want to improve your physical fitness, with all its advantages for your strength, stamina, bone density, resistance to disease, stress management and overall feelings of well-being, then my advice is to look your resistance in the eye and face it down. As previously mentioned in Chapter 3 ("It is Not Unpleasant"), *there is nothing in and of itself about exercise that is unpleasant or arduous.* You *can* learn to love exercise. You really can, if you are willing to suspend the critical capacity of your conscious mind and establish creative thinking.

Change is *often* dependent on your ability to suspend the critical capacity of your conscious mind. If your conscious mind insists that exercise is unpleasant, you will do well to suspend that belief. It is one hundred percent your attitude about exercise that will determine whether you experience it as pleasant or unpleasant. I challenge you to participate in exercise. While actively engaged, I challenge you to ask yourself if you are capable of feeling the physical sensations of exercise and to define those sensations as vigorous, vibrant and good. I am confident, gentle reader, that if you are willing to suspend your conscious mind's insistence that exercise is drudgery; you will be capable of creative thinking about exercise. You will be capable of experiencing something new and wonderful: the pleasure of exercise.

Overall Health Maintenance

Your good mental attitude, along with an exercise regimen,
good nutrition and good sleep habits will combine
to form a powerful force in the direction
of good overall health.

Let us place exercise and fitness into a broader context of overall health maintenance. In order to attain and maintain optimal health, we probably need to attend to four factors:

1. Exercise
2. Nutrition
3. Sleep
4. A good mental attitude

Factors 2, 3 and 4 are the subjects of the next three chapters.

Chapter 16
Nutrition

To provide a full, comprehensive treatment of this topic would require ten to twenty volumes. I would not be capable of writing them. Moreover, by the time someone had written and published the ten to twenty volumes, many of the ideas in them would have been called into question by subsequent research and ideas. Rather than throw up our hands and conclude that it is hopeless to address this important but extremely challenging topic, let us consider a number of habits to encourage and habits to discourage. These ideas are based on current knowledge as well as an application of reasonable, logical inference.

Weight Loss: Eliminate Fats or Carbs?

First of all, let us explode the notion that you can establish a consistent lifestyle that will propel you toward fitness and a healthy weight by unnaturally restricting fats or carbohydrates. It is undeniable that many persons have achieved weight loss by eliminating fats. It is also undeniable that many persons have achieved weight loss by eliminating carbohydrates. However, nowhere has it been established that persons can maintain such a regimen, integrate it with a realistic lifestyle, and maintain weight loss and optimal health for an extended period.

Protein, fats and carbohydrates are all necessary components of a healthy diet. They all have vital roles to play in the functioning of our bodies.

Protein is an important component of every cell in the body. On a genetic level, protein creates the scaffolding that maintains RNA molecules. Hair and nails are mostly made of protein. Your body uses protein to build and repair tissues. You also use protein to make enzymes, hormones, and other body chemicals. Protein is an important building block of bones, muscles, cartilage, skin, and blood.

Along with fat and carbohydrates, protein is a "macronutrient," meaning that the body needs relatively large amounts of it. Vitamins and minerals, which are needed in only small quantities, are called "micronutrients." But unlike fat and carbohydrates, the body does not store protein, and therefore has no reservoir on which to draw when it needs a new supply. Therefore, it is important to ingest protein every day.

Some good sources of protein:
- Boneless breast of chicken
- Broiled or baked fish
- Eggs
- Nuts
- Beans (when combined with whole grains or with any other source of complete protein).

- Dairy products such as yogurt, milk and cottage cheese (especially in low fat versions to minimize intake of animal fat).

Dietary fat is a nutrient that helps your body to absorb essential vitamins, maintain the structure and function of cell membranes, and help keep your immune system working. Mono-unsaturated fats are especially healthy because they lower the "bad cholesterol" (low density cholesterol, or LDL) in your blood. These mono-unsaturated fats include olive, canola, avocado, and nut oils. For optimal health, vegetable fats are usually preferable to animal fats.

Carbohydrates are the chemical means by which plants store the Sun's energy via photosynthesis. Animals store carbohydrates in the cells of their bodies in the form of lengthy chains called glycogen. When you breathe, you take in oxygen. Your body mixes some of the oxygen with carbon and hydrogen from carbohydrates. New compounds are formed – water and carbon dioxide – that you release to the environment when you exhale. Carbohydrates are a natural, necessary part of our existence.

The Mayo Clinic newsletter describes three main types of carbohydrates:

- Sugar: Sugar is the simplest form of carbohydrate. Sugar occurs naturally in some foods, including fruits, vegetables, milk and milk products. Sugars include fruit sugar (fructose), table sugar (sucrose) and milk sugar (lactose).

- Starch: Starch is a complex carbohydrate, meaning it is made of many sugar units bonded together. Starch occurs naturally in vegetables, grains, and cooked dry beans and peas.

- Fiber: Fiber is also a complex carbohydrate. Fiber occurs naturally in fruits, vegetables, whole grains, and cooked dry beans and peas.

Common, healthy sources of naturally occurring carbohydrates include fruits, vegetables, dairy products, nuts, grains and seeds. If we are to maintain healthy weight and a consistent energy flow, it is advantageous for us to restrict our intake of refined sugar.

Food Regimen Supportive
of Health and Fitness

The 80 – 20 Rule

The 80-20 rule is the idea that if you devote eighty percent of your time and energy to a healthy regimen, then you can be flexible the remaining twenty percent of the time. First, it is not realistic to expect perfection in any endeavor, even one as important as healthy nutrition. Regardless of the degree to which you consider good nutrition important, do you expect that you will **never** have a hamburger or a hot dog at a summer cookout? Do you expect that you will **never** have a piece of cake at someone's birthday celebration? Do you expect that you will **never** eat a high-fat or high-carbohydrate food to please a host?   Rather than to expect perfection, consider a standard that, while guiding you toward a food regimen supportive of health and fitness, will nevertheless have sufficient flexibility to allow for circumstances, lack of perfection, and occasional indulgences. If you can stay on a healthy nutritional regimen eighty percent of the time, you may decide to consider that to be success.

Ten Foods to emphasize
- Green, leafy vegetables
- Yellow vegetables
- Fruit
- Fish
- Boneless, skinless breast of chicken
- Beans, including lentils
- Whole grains (e.g. 100% whole grain breads, quinoa, brown rice)
- Unsalted nuts (particularly almonds, Brazil nuts, walnuts and pistachios)
- Chickpeas
- Low-fat dairy, such as yogurt

Ten foods to minimize
- Red meat
- Refined sugar (candy, pastry, pudding, most desserts)

- Cheese
- Refined, white flour (cake, donuts, white bread)
- Sweetened cereals
- Saturated fats
- Fried foods
- Poultry with skin on
- Soda
- Fatty sauces and dressings

These lists are not universally applicable. For instance, though low-fat dairy foods and whole grain breads are listed among foods to be emphasized, this does not apply to everyone. Some persons are better served by a dietary regimen avoiding dairy and wheat. Seek guidance and use your own best judgment in formulating your own plan.

Chapter 17
Sleep

Sleep is one of the great mysteries of human evolution and human functioning. We spend approximately one-third of our lives asleep, and science cannot confidently tell us why we do. The simplest and most obvious answer to the question of the function of sleep would be that sleep is restorative. But, of what is sleep restorative? A growing body of thought and evidence indicates that sleep is needed to maintain optimal functioning of the brain.

It is axiomatic that "the brain controls the body." The body is enervated by nervous tissue that originates in the spinal cord. And at the top of the spinal cord and directing most of the nerve activity is the brain. The brain accounts for approximately two percent of our body weight, yet is consumes twenty percent of our energy. It is "a very expensive organ" in terms of energy use. Unlike the muscles in the periphery of our body, the brain can only derive its energy from glycogen. Glycogen consists of long chains of glucose molecules, and is stored in the liver, muscles and brain cells. Glycogen is the body's fuel, and is used during muscular exertion. When glycogen stores are low in the body's periphery, we can burn fats. And when fat supplies run low, we can burn protein. The brain has no such luxury. It is glycogen or nothing. And if it is nothing, we cease to live.

I am promoting the idea that there are four components of a healthy lifestyle: exercise, nutrition, sleep and a good mental attitude. Sleep holds a prominent position in this foursome. The health consequences of inadequate nutrition or exercise, or of a poor mental attitude, may take a long time to develop. But several days without sleep can prove to be deadly.

Homeostasis is the property of the body by which variables are regulated with the purpose of maintaining stable internal conditions. For example, our bodies have systems to regulate temperature, blood sugar, blood oxygen and the balance between acidity and alkalinity, as well as many others. Sleep is a homeostatically regulated body function. We develop a "sleep debt" if we do not get the sleep the body requires. Our brains will work very hard to force us to pay back that sleep debt. The phenomenon of people falling asleep at the wheel or while in charge of important machines is a result of forced payment of a sleep debt.

The effects of sleep deprivation are many, and include:
- Moodiness
- Depression
- Yawning
- Impaired thinking
- Memory problems
- Weakened immune system
- High blood pressure
- Heart disease
- Weight gain
- Type II diabetes
- Fatigue
- Accidental death

Sleep, Energy and Memory

Most readers know that nerve cells called "neurons" conduct nerve impulses in the brain. What is less commonly known is that there are far more glial cells in the brain than there are neurons. Glial cells have a variety of functions, including providing neuronal axons with the myelin sheaths that speed up nerve conduction. Crucially, glial cells also store glycogen, and the steady supply of glycogen is essential for life. It is possible that sleep is a necessary component of the body's process of storing glycogen in the glial cells in the brain.

In addition, sleep serves the purpose of consolidating memory. There are two major types of memory: declarative and non-declarative memory. The two types of declarative memory are episodic memory and semantic memory. Episodic memory, as the term suggests, is memory of events, or episodes. Your memory that you worked out by lifting weights at the fitness center on Saturday, and that on Sunday you went kayaking, are examples of episodic memory. Semantic memory refers to general knowledge. Your memory that that there are three major branches of the United States government is an example of sematic memory. Your memory that the cell walls throughout your body depend on fat in your diet for their maintenance is another example of semantic memory.

There are apparently a number of types of non-declarative memory. Procedural memory is an important one, and one worth a comment here. As the name suggests, procedural memory is the memory of "how to" – of procedures. This is a more unconscious type of memory. How to type, to play a piece on the piano, to turn your baseball glove to backhand a ground ball, and to do a push-up or a crunch are all examples of procedural memory. There is a large body of experimental evidence showing that procedural memory is stronger when the learner has opportunity to sleep after first learning a new skill.

It should be obvious that maintaining good sleep patterns is essential for learning, health and fitness. But, what can we do when the demands of our stimulating and complicated lives impair our ability to fall asleep and to sleep restfully? Following are some suggestions.

Improving Sleep Patterns

There is a range of strategies to overcome difficulty falling asleep or sleeping through the night. You are not likely to use all of them. But it will help to *consider all the suggestions*, and then to select some to use. The effect of sleeplessness on your energy, concentration, resistance to illness, and feeling of well-being deserves attention. The following suggestions are organized into four categories:

A. Overall self-maintenance.
B. Patterns of rest and sleep.
C. Bedtime ritual.

D. Strategies for when you do not fall asleep.

A. Strategies involving your overall self-maintenance:

1.   Set aside a specific time each day to schedule your tasks and obligations.

2.   Learn a relaxation technique such as progressive muscle relaxation, deep breathing, Tai Chi, Yoga, or meditation. Practice the technique daily.

3.   Exercise regularly. Your exercise should be consistent with your physical condition and/or limitations. Brisk walking, swimming, and bicycling are all excellent exercises. Exercise at least three, and preferably five, times per week. Make it a priority.

4.   Do not overuse stimulants such as coffee, soda, chocolates, and cigarettes as these substances over-stimulate the nervous system.

5.   If you need help with bad habits, unresolved emotions or feeling disorganized, seek help from a psychotherapist. This does not make you weak. It makes you a willing problem-solver.

B. Strategies involving your patterns of rest and sleep:

1.   Use your bed only for sleep. Do not eat, study, or worry in bed. Reserve your bed for sleep so you will strongly associate bed and sleep.

2.   For most persons and for most purposes, it is best to avoid daytime naps. Naps diminish your need for

nighttime sleep, and reinforce irregular sleep patterns. As long as you are awake, your body is building up a homeostatic need for non-REM sleep. Daytime naps will discharge this homeostatic need, and may make it more difficult for you to sleep at night.

3. Establish the same rising time every morning. Do not even vary this by more than an hour or two on weekends. This will establish a rhythmic pattern that will help ensure that you will be sleepy at night so you can be regular in your pattern of wakefulness and sleep.

4. Make your bedroom attractive and comfortable. Reduce noises and lights, and maintain a comfortable room temperature.

5. Be sure your bed and mattress are comfortable and well suited to you.

C. Strategies involving a bedtime ritual:

1. Lie down to sleep only when you feel sleepy. Do not let yourself associate lying in bed with wakefulness, restlessness, and worry.

2. Use the last 15 - 30 minutes before bedtime for a pre-bed ritual. Included activities may be: shower, put on night clothes, brush teeth, make tomorrow's lunch, or listen to relaxing music.

3. Avoid stimulants for the 4 hours preceding bedtime. Vigorous exercise can be a stimulant, so it may be best to plan your regular exercise earlier in the day.

4. Avoid heavy meals before bed. A glass of milk or a small serving of yogurt (food containing calcium) may be helpful. Alcohol is not helpful, as it may cause initial drowsiness but often leads to disturbed sleep and frequent awakenings.

5. When you go to bed, assume a comfortable position, close your eyes, and use a relaxation method. Imagine a pleasant, relaxing scene, such as lying on a beach, and experience this imagery with all your senses. Think about what drowsiness, heaviness, and sleepiness feel like. Keep your eyes closed and avoid looking at the clock.

D. Strategies for times when you do not fall asleep:

1. When you first realize you are not dropping off to sleep, try to avoid self-defeating thoughts such as "It's happening again," or "I'll never sleep." Try to take a matter-of-fact attitude. Think, "As long as I lie comfortably with my eyes closed, I am allowing my eyes and body to rest, and my body is building up its homeostatic need for sleep. Sleep is inevitable."

2. If restlessness ensues or sleeplessness continues, rise and return to bed later when you are sleepy. When you rise, go to another room and occupy yourself with boring or monotonous tasks. Avoid pleasurable or exciting activities such as eating or drinking. If you read, choose something that will *not* remind you of work, school, politics, economics or social issues.

3.   If restlessness ensues after returning to bed, repeat the above procedure as needed.

4.   NOTE: Persistent insomnia may require medication. Although there is a risk that medication may be habit forming, this risk may be outweighed by the risk to your health and well-being of continued disrupted sleep. The drugs used in over-the-counter sleep medications have been demonstrated to be safe, but may not be effective. If you feel you need medicine, consult a physician and agree on a strategy.

E.   **A Special Note about Bedtime Reading**

Many practitioners recommend against bedtime reading. I recommend a different approach. If you do read before sleep, do not read any suspenseful fiction, as this may motivate you to remain awake "to see what happens." In addition, do not read anything that will remind you of work, school, politics, economics, social issues or commerce. You may well ask, "What is left?" *Answer:* ***Read about the natural world.*** This is a perfect time to read about astronomy, earth science, dinosaurs, rocks and shells, or the oceans. These topics are fascinating, but not in the same way as a suspenseful novel. Since the information you read will typically be new to you, it has a tendency to tire your mind, without drawing your attention to the types of topics that could stimulate worry or rumination (work, school, politics, economics, social issues or commerce).

Chapter 18
"A Good Mental Attitude"

First of all, gentle reader, I must admit that when I use the phrase "a good mental attitude," this is somewhat tongue-in-cheek. The expression "a good mental attitude" is something I expect to see in an article on healthy living in a magazine in the pocket of the seatback in front of me on an airplane. Nonetheless, a healthy emotionality is of utmost importance. The tongue-in-cheek expression "a good mental attitude" could include the following abilities:

- To attain physical relaxation.
- To be able to see things from the point of view of other persons and not just from our own perspective.
- To see the world in terms of "shades of grey" and not in absolutistic, black/white, all-or-nothing terms.
- To avoid catastrophic thinking.
- To have a sense of proportion about the importance of people, events and material things.
- To have a value system that makes sense.
- To be open to new ideas, while maintaining a healthy skepticism about ideas that have little basis in reality.
- To be able to renew the fascination with the natural world that we probably had as children, and
- To promote joy and contentment by consciously practicing principles for happiness.

This could easily be the topic of a dozen books. However, as this is a book primarily about fitness, I will limit the topic of maintaining a good mental attitude to the first and last of the above-listed items:

- Accentuate the positive with Fifteen Principles for Happiness;
- A way to attain deep physical relaxation.

Accentuate the Positive with Fifteen Principles for Happiness

Have you ever had the experience of witnessing something that made you feel very lucky? One typical example cited by many people is feeling grateful and happy to have two sound legs after seeing someone in a wheel chair. Another typical example is feeling grateful and happy to live in a country in which freedoms are relatively well protected when we hear about violation of civil rights or personal rights in a less democratic nation. Almost everyone has these experiences, and everyone reports a similar experience: feelings of luck, gratitude and happiness do arise, but soon fade away.

There are many experiences that give us a moment of perspective in which our own condition in life seems good, resulting in a feeling of increased happiness. The purpose of the method of **Fifteen Principles for Happiness** is to provide you with a ready-made set of perspectives to help you to re-create those moments of increased happiness. Please read the fifteen principles described below, and then the suggestions at the end.

ONE. It is all a bonus. Many people report that they have experienced a narrow escape from death. In particular, many people can remember "close calls" on the highway. In addition, we have all heard accounts of seemingly healthy persons dying suddenly from such causes as heart attacks or aneurisms. If you have ever had a narrow escape from death, then you know that, in a sense, you are fortunate just to be alive. Therefore, regardless of what happens in your life today, tell yourself that any sense of pleasure you have is a bonus. Every moment of contentment or pleasure is more than you would have had if you were no longer alive.

TWO. It is not my world; it is the world. This is a particularly good principle for persons who are socially conscious. Have you ever looked at the world around you and felt distressed by greed, corruption or violence? When you feel unhappy or frustrated about the state of things in the world around you, protect yourself from any sense of personal failure. Do not take it personally that we do not have a better world. You do have one citizen's responsibility, but that is all. It is, after all, **not** your world, but just *the world*.

THREE. Humor and laughter: Have you ever been in a difficult situation, and you or someone with you said, "Someday we'll look back on this and laugh"? Why wait? Laugh now, if you can. Admittedly, there is often nothing truly funny in a light-hearted sense about the difficulty.

Maybe it is only "funny" in that it is absurd. Even if the only humor you can see in the situation is the humor of the absurd, try to see that humor.

FOUR. Do you remember January of 1991? It was the start of Operation Desert Storm - the Persian Gulf War. Have you ever wondered what it would have felt like to have been in occupied Kuwait during the Persian Gulf War? If you do not recall that event, it is certain that you can think of some other event in which the people involved were living with terror. If you can imagine what it would feel like to be in a truly terrifying situation, then regardless of what you have to face today, it is probably not too bad when seen in that perspective.

FIVE. Picture a group of hikers out for a walk. A bee hive is disturbed and a small swarm of bees comes out and they sting . . . one hiker. Why that one?!? Answer: random. We all get some bad luck, and it is best not to take it personally when you get yours. It is best not to feel as though life, fate or nature has ganged up on you personally. When you have bad luck, tell yourself it is your random share. Try to solve the problem and move on without thinking that fate or nature "has it in for you."

SIX. Imagine a hospital patient, on his deathbed, dying of stress related disease. He looks at his bedside table before dying and sees a glass of water - half full. Before dying, he smiles ruefully to himself and says, "Here I am, dying of stress related disease, because I spent my entire life seeing that glass as half empty instead of half full." It is best to accept the fact that the glass will always be half empty - that there will always be imperfections in your life. But there are always some aspects of your life that can make you feel happier - if you will let yourself notice them and enjoy them.

SEVEN. If there is such a thing as heaven on Earth, it comes when we are fully aware that life is a process and not a product. Your life is not a resume . . . not a portfolio . . . not a house under construction. The expression "my life is ruined" is possible only when we feel life is a product instead of what it is in reality - a succession of moments for us to experience.

EIGHT. Imagine a big wrought iron gate and fence. Inside the fence is a park in which people are very happy, playing, singing, and relaxing. A person is trying to climb over the gate and into the park, but cannot make it because s/he is carrying excess baggage. The baggage consists of the demands and expectations of the (dead) past and the (imagined) future. We can make it into the happy park as long as we can prevent our consciousness from being dominated by the demands and expectations of the dead past and the imagined future.

NINE. If we want to drink the wine of life with any gusto, it probably takes some hard work and self-discipline. No one has ever achieved optimal human happiness by just sitting around trying to passively enjoy him or herself without effort or commitment.

TEN.   Imagine a den of lions eating their kill. The operant word here is "kill," or death. We will all die. Between now and then we will have many feelings, and we have a right to all of them, no matter what they are. However, if we are often immersing ourselves in certain negative feelings such as feeling put down, put upon, cheated, angry, hateful, deprived, et cetera, we may want to ask ourselves how much of our precious time we want to devote to those feelings.

ELEVEN. Imagine a quarterback whose team is pushed all the way back to his own 2-yard line. He desperately wants to score a touchdown, so he keeps throwing long passes. The defense, sensing what is happening, defends easily, and the quarterback fails. If, seeing the defense playing deep, he had been content to throw short passes, our quarterback may have picked up 6, 8, or 10 yards every play. The point: take what the defense gives you.   And, be satisfied with small steps of progress toward your ultimate goals and desires if, as is often the case, you cannot achieve them all at once.

TWELVE.   Imagine a trophy shelf with all the trophies signifying a person's accomplishments.   But they are all jumbled in together and look like a mess. On the wall nearby is a simple, elegant plaque that states that this person has reasonable values . . . and lives by them. In the final analysis we are probably happiest if we know who we are - know what we value - and live accordingly.

THIRTEEN. Imagine a person with a sprained wrist. He wanted to do carpentry that day, but cannot. First, he bandages the wrist, but then immediately turns his attention to other activities that he can enjoy without use of his wrist. The point: do not ignore the parts of your life that are going poorly. Take at least one-step toward improving things. Then consider turning your attention to matters that are going well and that can bring you some happiness now.

FOURTEEN. Imagine two lovers on a park bench. But they are not busy courting; they are staring at some people doing Tai Chi in the park. Tai Chi, an eastern martial art form, involves slow, elegant motions, and many individuals practice it in parks. Use this image as a reminder that we are happier and more efficient when we do things in a moderately paced, well-considered, elegant way than when we do things in a rushed, hectic, frenzied way. *Avoid frenzy*!

FIFTEEN. Imagine a weight lifter, looking in the mirror and comparing himself to other weight lifters. The idea here has to do with comparisons. When we compare ourselves to others, we get one of two results. Either we judge ourselves superior and feel vain, or we judge ourselves inferior and feel deprived. Neither feeling will make us happy. Some comparisons are inevitable, but it will be in our better interest to limit them if we can.

Suggestions

1. Review all fifteen principles twice a day for two days.

2. After the second day, select a shorter list of five to seven of the principles that seem most meaningful to you.

3. Continue to review your selected list twice a day. Give the ideas a chance to sink in to the point that you can feel them intuitively or "in your gut." It is not enough to just repeat the words (e.g. "It's all a bonus . . . . . yeah, it's a bonus"). Stay with the thoughts until you can really feel their effects. Just one of these principles can lift your spirits at any given moment. Principle #9 emphasizes that happiness takes some hard work and self-discipline. Work conscientiously at this exercise and . . . feel happier.

Attaining Deep Physical Relaxation

The method I will describe for you is called progressive relaxation. This method has been around, as far as the western world is concerned, since the early part of last century, when a physiologist named Edmund Jacobson devised it. Jacobson was a physiologist who worked at places such as Harvard, Cornell and Bell Laboratories. He was interested in what happens to people physically and medically when they say that they are nervous, tense and worked up. He and researchers since him have found some very interesting things. Every major system of the body is affected. The muscular-skeletal system is affected in that individual muscle fibers are shorter and tighter. Because those individual muscle fibers are shorter and tighter, there is increased activity in the nervous tissue that serves those muscles. Thus, the nervous system is affected. Because individual muscle fibers are shorter and tighter, the muscles want more oxygen, so the respiratory system is affected. Since oxygen is delivered to the muscles through the bloodstream, the circulation system is affected. There is an increase in both blood pressure and heart rate. The endocrine system is affected, with an increased secretion of adrenaline into the bloodstream, which by the way, is a primary feature of a panic attack. The digestive system is affected, with an increased secretion of digestive acids. The integumentary system, which most of us call the skin, is affected in that there is an increase in skin conductance. And, some people get rashes such as hives or eczema when they are tense. Even the immune system is affected. T-lymphocyte cells fight infection, recruit B-cells to further fight infection, and induce a cascade of reactions on the part of the human immune system. However, these immune system reactions are less active and less available when we are tense. In summary, every major system of the body is affected by physical tension.

To practice progressive relaxation, we first set aside fifteen minutes, and we find a place in which we can be comfortable and in which we will be undisturbed for fifteen minutes. The very process of ensuring that we will be undisturbed can pay dividends. I have had adults tell me that insisting on fifteen minutes of undisturbed time changed the dynamics in their homes. Their children had to adjust to the fact that they were not the Centre of the Universe one hundred percent of the time. They learned that that Mom or Dad has needs and rights, too. All by itself, insisting on the time to practice relaxation is an exercise in reducing distractions and behaving more purposefully.

Progressive relaxation is such a fine technique that even a mediocre practice of it can have a desirable effect. However, I recommend having a well-refined, excellent way of practicing the technique. When we are first learning it, the technique takes about fifteen minutes. Jacobson wanted to find one of the afore-mentioned physical changes that could come under some voluntary control, so he chose the shortening of muscle fibers. In order to lengthen the muscle fibers and to induce an array of other reactions, we first tense, and then release, muscles throughout the body.

In our day-to-day lives we can become so involved with what is going on in our minds that we can totally lose touch with what is going on in our bodies. If you think about it, I am sure you will agree. Perhaps you can remember driving your car, and stopping for a break. Only at the break did you realize that you were driving all tensed up. Tension can build up without our even knowing it.

The pages that follow will include step-by-step directions, just as I use in session to instruct a patient to relax. You may wish to read and record these directions for yourself. You may want to have a companion read them to you. Alternatively, you could simply familiarize yourself with the directions and perform the exercises from memory.

Find a comfortable position in which to perform your relaxation exercise. If you lie down on a sofa or a bed, ensure that your back, neck and head are in a comfortably aligned position. If you are seated in a chair, make sure your feet can rest flat on the floor and that your hands and arms are in a comfortable and well-supported position. Your next preparation for the exercise is to take a few slow, deep breaths, exhaling naturally. You want your abdomen to rise and fall with each breath. When your abdomen rises with an inhalation, your diaphragm descends, and your lungs can fill more fully. If you are not sure you are breathing in this way, place the palm of one hand on your abdomen and take a few breaths. Some people suck in their stomachs and expand their chests when they inhale. That is not as relaxing a way to breathe, and does not allow the lungs to fill as well with air. If you are in fact breathing that way, take a few moments to practice deep breathing with your abdomen rising as you inhale.

You are now ready to go through the body, one major muscle group at a time. When you put tension in, do not use all your strength or anything resembling it. Just put in a moderate amount of tension. And when you let the tension go, let it go all at once. You will go through your body one muscle group at a time. You will put in moderate tension, and will let tension go all at once. You will be taking a few slow, deep breaths, focusing your attention in certain, special ways and enjoying your resulting relaxation.

Begin with a slow, deep breath . . . . . and, let go. Again, take a slow, deep breath. . . and let go. Make sure that you are allowing your abdomen to rise and fall with each breath.

Now, remembering to use just a moderate amount of tension, make your right hand into a fist. Just be aware of what that tension is like, take a deep breath, and hold it . . . and, let go. Stretch your fingers out wide and, let them fall back into a natural, relaxed position. Your right hand may feel a little warm or tingly. Take a slow, deep breath. . . . and, let go.

Same hand . . . make your right hand into a fist, and straighten your right arm, putting tension all the way to your shoulder. Take a deep breath, and hold it . . . . . and, exhale and let go. Stretch the fingers wide, and let them relax. Pay careful attention to the difference between the tight, tense feeling and the relaxed feeling. The more aware we are of the difference between these feelings the more easily we can let go . . . and the more fully we can relax. Take a slow, deep breath . . . and let go. Pause for a moment as you let yourself become fully aware of the difference between the tense feelings and the relaxed feelings. The next will be the last time for the right hand and the right arm. Make your right hand into a fist and straighten . . . moderate tension . . . hold it . . . and, exhale and let go. Stretch your fingers out wide . . .

. . and, let them fall into a natural position. Let your imagination help. Imagine any remaining tension draining down your right arm and out through the fingertips of your right hand.

Already you have learned a lot about how much tension you have to introduce in order for you to then fully appreciate, and fully enjoy, the feeling of relaxation. With that in mind, you will go to the left side. Do not introduce any more tension than you have to. Make your left hand into a fist. Put your mind and your awareness into that left hand and become fully acquainted with that tense feeling. Take a breath and hold it . . . and, exhale and let go. Stretch the fingers . . . and let them go.

With every muscle group that you work on you are going to feel more relaxed. With every muscle group you work on you are going to feel more calm.

Now make your left hand into a fist, and straighten your left arm. Introduce moderate tension all the way to the shoulder. Take a breath and hold it . . . and exhale and let go. Stretch the fingers, and let them go. Be aware of what it feels like as the tension that you put in fades away. Be aware of what it feels like as relaxation takes over. Now this will be the last time for the left hand and the left arm. Make your left hand into a fist and straighten . . . moderate tension . . . take a breath and hold it . . . and, exhale and let go.

Stretch the fingers . . . and let them relax. Notice the difference between tightness and relaxation. Just as with the right side, let your imagination help. Imagine any remaining tension draining down your left arm and out through the fingertips of your left hand.

Now draw your shoulders up as though you were going to pull them up around your ears. Take a breath and hold it. Feel that tension . . . exhale, and let go. Let your shoulders enjoy the feeling that they are sinking down as deeply as they want to go. Let go a little more, and relax a little more. You will be surprised, and pleased, at how relaxed you can be. Make sure at this point that your hands and arms are in a comfortable, well-supported position.

In the muscles of the face you are going to introduce only a very small amount of tension – just enough for you to appreciate and enjoy the feeling of relaxation. We will start with the forehead. See if you can put a little tension in by gently knitting your eyebrows . . . and relax. Now gently raise your eyebrows . . . and relax. Feel what your forehead feels like as the tension that you put in fades away . . . and as relaxation takes over.

Now close your eyes and very slowly, very gradually, close your eyes a little bit tighter . . . and relax. You can allow your eyes to remain closed. Allow your forehead, your eyes, and your eyelids to all feel comfortable . . . perhaps a little heavy . . . and relaxed. Gently press your tongue against the roof of your mouth . . . and relax. Take a slow, deep breath . . . and . . . let go.

Place your teeth together in a good, firm, comfortable bite. Slowly, gradually, bite down a little harder, until you can feel some tension in your jaw . . . and . . . relax. As though you were very sleepy and had to yawn, open your mouth very wide like a big, wide yawn. And . . . relax. Allow your lips to remain a little bit apart, and feel what your face and your jaw feel like as the tension, and any tingling sensation that you introduced, fades away. Take a moment to notice the difference in the way you feel now compared to when you started.

Straighten your right leg, bringing your heel off the floor. Draw your toes back, stretching your calf muscle . . . and relax. Gently draw your right leg back just far enough for your foot to rest flat on the floor. Feel what your right leg feels like as the tension, and any tingling sensation that you introduced, fades away. Now straighten your left leg. Draw your toes back, stretching your calf muscle . . .   and relax. Gently draw your left leg back, and feel what your left leg feels like as the tension, and any tingling sensation, fades away.

The last muscle group that you will add any tension to will be the abdomen. Take a breath and tighten your abdomen . . . hold it . . . and . . . exhale and let go. Continue to breathe normally. Be aware of what your abdomen feels like as it gently rises and falls with each breath. With every breath that you exhale, allow yourself to let go a little more. With every breath that you exhale, allow yourself to relax even more.

Think the following words: peaceful . . . calm . . . and serene. Imagine yourself saying those three words out loud . . . peaceful, calm and serene. You may find that you have a preference for one of the three. In your mind, select your favorite. And, in your mind only, without using your lips or your voice, think that word to yourself as you exhale. Do this for your next few breaths.

You have completed the tense/release portion of the relaxation exercise. The next instructions are for what I call "the focusing method." Draw your attention to your forehead and your eyes and let your forehead and eyes relax completely. Really let go throughout your forehead and eyes, and imagine the tiny muscles there becoming smooth and relaxed. Let your face and your jaw relax. Focus on a sense of stillness, like a pond without a ripple. Let your neck and your shoulders relax. Focus on a sense of letting go. And, as you let go throughout your neck and your shoulders, imagine the muscles there becoming smooth and relaxed. Let your right arm and your right hand relax, knowing, as you do now, that relaxation is a skill . . . knowing that you can acquire and then develop the skill of relaxation . . . knowing that in so doing you will be increasing your sense of self control . . . and knowing that increased self-control will improve your self confidence. Let your left arm and your left hand relax. Imagine any remaining tension draining down your left arm and out through the fingertips of your left hand. Let your entire upper body relax, including your shoulders, back and abdomen. Imagine tension leaving your body the way air might leave a deflating air mattress. Let the rest of your body relax, including your legs and your feet. As you each exhale each of your next few breaths, repeat to yourself the word that you selected – peaceful, calm or serene.

Imagine any remaining tension draining out of your muscles the way water might drain through a pipe, leaving your muscles smooth and relaxed. Let your shoulders feel that they are sinking down as deeply as they want to go, leaving your hands and arms heavy and relaxed. Focus on a sense of letting go, leaving you with a sense of stillness, like a pond without a ripple.

Continue to relax for a few more moments, and tell yourself the following:

• At this moment you have no obligations other than to relax.

• In the week ahead you will retain a clear memory of the way you feel now, and even that memory will help you.

• Every time you practice relaxation you will succeed, and you will become more skilled with practice. If you relax before sleeping, you will sleep more peacefully and therefore, of course, you will awaken more refreshed.

• Even more importantly, if you relax soon after rising, it will help you begin your waking period more relaxed. That will make you so much more aware of what tension feels like at its earliest noticeable onset, that you may be able to prevent its build-up in the first place. That will be a great accomplishment, and a savings of energy – energy that would otherwise be squandered in nervous tension.

• Something will happen this week . . . something that might ordinarily make you feel nervous or rattled. But you will feel less nervous than usual. You will deal with it. You will find a solution. You may even feel that you have shed a bit of unpleasantness from about you the way you would shed rain from an umbrella. And that will feel good.

• When you conclude the exercise and open your eyes, you will still feel relaxed, and you will also feel alert, refreshed, and with a sense of well being. You will also be very much aware that you can develop your own internal skills to help yourself.

That concludes the progressive relaxation exercise. You may want to read the entire description as it is written on these pages before performing the exercise, and then to do the exercise by memory. A second method would be for you to read the transcript aloud and to record it for yourself. You would then be able to play it back for yourself as you perform the exercise. A third method would be to have another person read the instructions for you as you learn the technique. Regardless of which way you choose to acquire the skill of relaxation, you will find deep relaxation to be an enormous help in quieting your body and mind in such a way as to set the stage for more organized thoughts and actions. Following is a review of the recommended use of the progressive relaxation method that has been described.

Review of Progressive Relaxation

Set aside 15 minutes, and try to ensure you will be left undisturbed.

Sit comfortably in a chair, or recline, or lie down. If you sit up, place your feet flat on the floor and be sure your hands and arms are comfortably supported. If you are reclining or lying down, be sure your head, neck and back are comfortably aligned.

Experience the difference between tense and relaxed feelings by tensing and then relaxing muscles, as has been described. Introduce only as much tension as you need. After you have applied tension, take a breath and hold it for 3-5 seconds. Let go of tension all at once, as you exhale your breath. Do not hold your breath while working on the muscles of your face and head. Apply this procedure to your hands, hands and arms, shoulders, forehead, eyes, tongue, jaw, legs and abdomen.

After releasing tension, take a few moments to really feel and appreciate the difference between tense and relaxed feelings.

THE FOCUSING METHOD: Draw your attention to each muscle group again, one at a time. This time introduce no tension. Rather, just allow relaxation to deepen in one of the following ways:

- Imagine your muscles becoming smooth and relaxed.
- Imagine tension draining out of your muscles, the way water might drain through a pipe.
- Imagine tension leaving your body the way air might escape a deflating air mattress.
- Just focus on a sense of letting go.

Now and then, throughout the exercise, take a slow, deep breath and let it go. As you exhale, think your choice of the following three words: "peaceful, calm, or serene."

Practice these exercises three times per day. The purpose of these exercises is to build your skill of relaxation – not just to help soften a stress-filled week. Practice the exercise regardless of whether you are having an easy or a difficult week.

If you will work on accentuating the positive by using Principles for Happiness, and will practice progressive relaxation, you will have acquired two very important tools for attaining and maintaining a good mental attitude. Your good mental attitude, along with an exercise regimen, good nutrition and good sleep habits will combine to be a powerful force in the direction of good overall health.

Chapter 19
What is the best fitness program for me?

*The most important consideration for you is to devise
a fitness regimen that you will be able to start
and with which you can persist.*

I have a resounding answer to this question. *The best program for you is the one at which you can persist* for the foreseeable future. It would be easy to say the following:

- Your best program needs to include some resistance training for strength and bone density.
- Your best program needs to have aerobic training to optimize your heart and lung efficiency.
- Your best program needs to include stretching, to help prevent cramps and to make you less subject to injuries such as strains or muscle tears.
- Your best program needs to include balance training to make you less prone to accidents.
- Your best program needs to include mind-body integration, to help you reduce physical tension, and to optimize your health holistically.
- Your best program needs to include core stability training.

However, most individuals are, for one reason or another, not going to maintain a comprehensive fitness program including the six components listed above. While it is important for you to consider the six types of training listed above, the most important factor of all is that you partake in at least some fitness regimen. Keep in mind that a very small regimen in one domain is better than no fitness program at all. When push comes to shove, the most important consideration for you is to devise a fitness regimen that you will be able to start and with which you can persist. For instance, a fitness regimen that includes thirty minutes of exercise three times per week, and to which you adhere week after week, is worth much more than a regimen of an hour of exercise five times a week that is quickly abandoned.

My hope for readers is that your fitness regimen will be an exercise in self-enhancement and not one of self-oppression.

Chapter 20
The Motivation Factor

When you are able to lessen your self-demands and to learn not to be your own most severe critic, you will find yourself at optimal arousal levels and able to achieve your best.

Everyone has desires and dreams. We have ideas about what would be a happy, satisfying life. For many individuals, being physically fit is among their desires. Subconsciously we may have created an entire set of images portraying physical fitness. Moreover, many individuals have specific goals that they have set for themselves in order to try to spur themselves on toward their dreams of an active, fit life.

Despite the existence of goals and dreams about fitness, a large percentage of people find themselves failing to put sufficient effort into the pursuit of their dreams. In effect, they appear to lack the motivation to succeed. Just what is this sometimes-elusive commodity . . . "motivation"?

Although in one sense, you may be motivated to exercise and to be fit, in another sense you may lack effective motivation. *Plain motivation* means just wanting to be fit. *Effective motivation* means being in the habit of organizing your life in certain ways - ways that will result in the following components being present in your thoughts and plans:

1.	Establishment of a goal regarding exercise and fitness
2.	Breaking the goal down into smaller, achievable steps
3.	Overcoming external blocks to goal - attainment
4.	Overcoming internal blocks to goal - attainment
5.	Seeking help in appropriate ways
6.	Anticipating future rewards

When you are able to plan things in this way - and to explicitly and unambiguously address these 6 components of effective motivation - you will find yourself accomplishing more.

Component #1
Establishing a Goal

It is not enough to say that a happy, satisfying life would include health and fitness. Moreover, it is not enough to have a set of images that portray those ideas. Most individuals need to be more specific in their thinking and planning in order to be effectively motivated.

When you select a goal, be sure that it is specific and definite enough for you to know when you have achieved it.

Definite Goals:
- I will begin walking two miles, three times per week.

- Within 2 months, I will begin running.
- Within 6 months, I will be running 2 miles in 15 minutes or less.

Make your goals specific enough for you to know when you have achieved them. And, set them at a reasonable difficulty level. Goals should be sufficiently challenging to be meaningful, but not so difficult as to be unattainable or likely to cause frustration.

Component #2
Breaking Goals down into Achievable Steps

This may be the most important component of effective motivation. When we look at tasks as a whole, they may seem formidable or complicated and we may back down from them. We may feel incapable of successfully completing tasks. At that moment, we are in danger of abandoning goals in despair before we have begun.

However, if we can break larger goals down into smaller sections, we no longer have to confront entire tasks. We need only address the first step. Tasks no longer appear overwhelming. We may complete the first step successfully and experience a sense of accomplishment. This gives us more energy for handling the second step, and so on. The process of task completion and goal attainment depends on getting started, and getting started often depends on setting up an achievable, non-formidable first step.

Examples of Setting up the First Few Achievable Steps of a Larger Task:

- I will go to a sporting goods store and will purchase a comfortable pair of running shoes.
- I will walk one-half mile, three times per week to be sure my new shoes are comfortable and to begin establishing the routine of walking.
- I will increase my walks from one-half mile to one mile.
- I will increase my walks to two-miles.

Component #3
Overcoming External Barriers to Goal Attainment

The road to goal attainment is strewn with obstacles. Some are of our own making, but many are not. There are external forces or factors that we must successfully negotiate if we are to succeed. These obstacles come in a great variety. They may be forces of nature, human laws or rules, other people's competing wishes, or actual physical obstacles. Whatever their nature, it is important that you identify them and make a plan to contend with them. Neglecting to do so could result in frustrated plans that can reduce that commodity we are discussing: motivation.

The following are examples of overcoming external blocks to goal attainment:

- Saving money on a regular basis to enable you to purchase a fitness center membership.
- Arranging for childcare to enable you enough time for a fitness regimen.
- Negotiating a work schedule that will allow sufficient time for workouts.

External blocks will often be present to at least some degree in situations when you strive to attain meaningful goals. Identifying those barriers as soon as possible, and making explicit plans to overcome them, will be an important part of your effective motivation.

Component #4
Overcoming Internal Barriers to Goal Attainment

The road to goal attainment is laden with obstacles, and some we create. To overcome these obstacles we need to identify them and describe them in a manner that makes them manageable. For instance, if I label myself "lazy," I create an obstacle by implying I am and always will be lazy in all situations. This is probably not true. Perhaps a more accurate statement would be: "When I cannot clearly imagine how to become fit, I stop trying, and this gives the appearance of laziness." The internal block to overcome in such an instance would not be "laziness," but rather "a tendency to stop working when goal-attainment cannot be imagined." You can make a plan for overcoming that obstacle. We can learn to create vivid images of goal-attainment, and we can remind ourselves to review those images now and then during our work. However, if we think the obstacle is the *trait of laziness*, then no concrete plans for resolving that problem can be made.

Component #5
Seeking Help in Appropriate Ways

Actually, component #5 is often practiced in conjunction with the other components, particularly 3 and 4. In many actual situations, overcoming barriers requires a combination of self-help and assistance from others.

Seeking help can be a difficult process for many individuals in our society. Many persons have a tendency toward "counterdependence." That is, they have no difficulty offering help *to* others, but feel very awkward about seeking or accepting assistance *from* others. This can be a very sad thing for them. We can experience a very satisfying feeling of human closeness and support when we accept help from others, but some people miss out on this feeling.

From a practical point of view, the total knowledge, skills, and experience needed to successfully negotiate this world is formidable. A reluctance to seek help from others when appropriate can be a significant handicap to effective goal-attainment and a happy life.

The following is an example of seeking help for purposes of goal attainment:

Linda had grown up with no knowledge or skills at establishing or maintaining a fitness regimen. She felt that this was a gap in her personal repertoire, and she wanted the skills to plan and carry out an exercise program. However, Linda was not asking for help because she was afraid of appearing dependent and stupid.

Finally, she discussed her dilemma with two friends who were fitness enthusiasts. She invited them for lunch, telling them that she would appreciate a few hours of time and some specific tips on how to set up her exercise program. She told them that she believed she would appear stupid but that she really needed help to get started. After receiving her friends' help, Linda bought the tools they had recommended. One friend visited and helped her assemble a small home workout center, and within a few months, Linda had begun a modest but significant program of light weight lifting and aerobic work on a stationary bicycle. She was experiencing a new sense of confidence, and was feeling great about herself. Requesting help from her friends was a crucial step in enabling Linda to attain her goal. It was the turning point of her effective motivation.

Component #6
Anticipating future rewards

Many goals that people set for themselves are long term. Therefore, an important component of effective motivation is maintaining drive and enthusiasm over the long haul. It is not unusual for a person to set a fitness goal and work hard, only to languish somewhere along the way and to leave the goal unreached. This is probably true more often than not. The *International Journal on Exercise and Fitness* has reported that fifty percent of persons who begin a fitness program abandon it within the first six months.

All five of the previously discussed components are important, with special emphasis on component #2 - breaking the goal down into smaller, achievable steps. However, even after seeking help when appropriate, overcoming external and internal barriers to goal-attainment, and achieving steps toward the goal, the human motivational apparatus can still break down. The final ingredient is to remind yourself occasionally of the ultimate goal of your efforts.

The rewards of attaining fitness goals vary from person to person. However, there are many common themes:

- Feeling generally stronger and more vital.
- Being more resistant to illness.
- Having a more attractive appearance.
- Hearing compliments from others.
- Participation in a sport or outdoor activity that requires a degree of strength or endurance.

Do not waste valuable workout time now by spending too much time imagining the future you will have once your goals are reached. However, do occasionally bring to mind an image of goal attainment and its rewards.

Becoming fit is a distance event, not a sprint. In a sprint, you can run into oxygen debt, because the event will be over in such a short time. But in a distance event you cannot run into oxygen debt. You must stay within your abilities and set a pace you can maintain.

The Motivation Paradox

Performance goes up as our level of arousal goes up . . . . to a point. Then, performance drops as arousal gets even higher. This phenomenon is known as the Yerkes-Dodson Law, and it has profound implications for us as we attempt to raise our efficiency and performance. The Yerkes-Dodson Law is typically described as a curve – like the top half of a circle.

According to the motivation curve, performance is very low when we are asleep or bored, and climbs to its highest point when we are at optimal arousal. However, as arousal and motivation continue to increase, performance drops. We get into a danger zone in which anxiety, high anxiety, and rigid self-demands actually decrease our performance. This is a difficult pill to swallow for most persons in our society, who tend to believe that we can drive ourselves to peak performance through rigid self-demands, and by being our own worst critic.

Search your memory and your experiences for a particular type of event that may convince you of the truth of the motivation curve. Have you ever practiced a skill that you sometimes performed at a function in front of an audience? Examples may include playing a musical instrument, being on a debating team, or playing athletics in a league. And, when performing in such a situation, did tightness or nervousness inhibit you somewhat? (When I give lectures on this topic, approximately eighty percent of the audience - males and females - typically answer affirmatively). Then, I ask, "Have you ever performed such an activity, such as softball or volleyball at a picnic, at which no team standings were at stake?" (Again, about eighty percent usually say "yes.") Finally . . . have you ever noticed that, while performing a skill in a relaxing setting with nothing at stake, you found yourself doing your very best? (Almost the entire eighty percent typically say that in fact they have found themselves being their very most artful and skillful while performing at the relaxing event). This is an apparent paradox. The less we tell ourselves that we "have to succeed," the more success we are likely to achieve.

What does this mean? Clearly, when there is something at stake or you are playing to win, your motivation is very high. You are, in effect, highly aroused, but your performance may suffer. You can actually see how performance declines for many people when they are highly aroused. There is a visible physical tightness that inhibits their most artful performance.

But why do you perform so well when nothing is at stake? Because you love it . . . that is why ! ! !

You love doing your best! It is intrinsically satisfying to experience a peak performance. This is true for almost all persons, whether the performance is artistic, athletic, social, vocational, or academic. That is all the motivation you need. Most people will achieve their peak performances when they are experiencing the thrill and satisfaction of performing an activity well. When you add in the anxiety of worrying about consequences, such as league standings, performances typically drop. Of course, there are those individuals, such as professional athletes, who perform their best under pressure. That is the exception and not the rule. When you are able to lessen your self-demands and to learn *not* to be your own toughest critic, you will find yourself at optimal arousal levels and able to achieve your best.

Chapter 21
Keeping it in Perspective

The "meaning of our health routines" is full and vital
participation in life and life activities.
Do not "lose the meaning" while
caught up in the ardor
of your workouts.

Fitness is a wonderful attribute to have. But is fitness the
ultimate goal in and of itself? Or is fitness part of an overall
effort to a have a rewarding life? Is there a greater goal, or a
greater set of greater goals?

I have at times promoted the ideas of major life goals and of
initiatives for happiness. Some of them are as follows:

- Health, vigor and physical activity
- Enjoying the beauty of nature
- Curiosity and wonder about the natural world
- Enjoyment of culture (art, music, literature, history)
- Joy
- Productivity
- Meaning
- Relationships

It may be helpful to think of fitness as being "in service of" goals such as those listed above. For instance, suppose you wanted to take a hike on a long or demanding nature trail to enjoy the beauty of nature and to learn about wildlife. Fitness would enable you to engage in that activity with greater comfort and for a longer amount of time. It would enable you to access environments that would be inaccessible to you if you were not fit.

Sometimes an individual can become so immersed in an exercise regimen that the original goals of doing so are forgotten. I recall working with a therapy patient (We will call him "Al") who had concerns about his wife (We will call her "Kim"). Kim had become very devoted to her fitness routine, and to her dietary regimen. Al enjoyed getting together with friends for dinner in restaurants, and Kim had always participated with enthusiasm. However, as she became increasingly devoted to her dietary regimen, she because reluctant to dine in restaurants. She ultimately refused to participate, complaining that she would be unable to follow her dietary plan. In addition, Kim's family had annual reunions in a location that afforded opportunity for camping, hiking and swimming. The reunions were not primarily athletic events, though there were opportunities for at least moderate physical exercise. Kim was reluctant to attend. She had been increasing the intensity of her gym workouts, and she stated, "Going to the reunion will interfere with the progress I am making in my gym workouts."

Al asked for my help in communicating to Kim in a way that would enable her to re-establish a more comfortable stance on these matters. I suggested to Al that he essentially tell Kim that she had "lost the meaning" of her efforts. Presumably, she had embarked on improved exercise and dietary routines to enhance her life. She wanted to live a long life, to stay healthy and active as long as possible, and to be sufficiently vigorous and fit to get full enjoyment out of such activities as her family reunion and dinners out with friends. Exercise and healthy dietary habits had started out as means to an end. The end was to have been full and vital participation in life. Somewhere along the way, while improving her exercise and dietary regimen, *the means had become the end*. The "meaning of her health routines" was to have been full and vital participation in life activities, but she had "lost the meaning" while caught up in the ardor of her efforts.

There are many examples of people starting out with a goal, choosing a means to attain that goal, and then letting the means become the goal. Think about someone buying a house in order to have a happy environment for a family. I know of instances in which they renovated and furnished the living room, then forbade their children from using the living room in order to retain it in a pristine condition. The living room, at first conceived as a means to happy family activity, took over as the end. Another very common example is an automobile. We purchase a car as a means to transport ourselves to work, and to social, and recreational events. Then many individuals wash, wax and protect their cars, perhaps even avoiding events that, though exciting, may be crowded or dusty. They may do this to avoid scratches, dents, dirt and dust from marring their car. The car has become more of an end than a means.

Physical fitness is a wonderful pursuit. I would not have put the effort into writing this book if I did not value fitness very highly. I urge you to be devoted to your health and fitness. However, I also urge you to be mindful of your ultimate goals in life. Feeling healthy, strong and vigorous is an admirable goal. But fitness workouts in and of themselves are not the goal. They are a means toward the goal. Keep your fitness regimen in its proper perspective. Do not allow your devotion to your exercise routine itself to preclude your attainment of other important life goals, or your participation in other life enhancing activities.

Chapter 22
Embrace Life and Fitness

*The longer we maintain our mental alertness, and the longer
we maintain our physical fitness, the greater will be
our joy and contentment in life.*

Forgive me, gentle reader, if I stray into the scientific and
philosophical realm, but I want you to experience joy and
wonder as well as fitness. I believe that an appreciation of
what the Universe has gone through to make our lives
possible can greatly enhance our lives. The Universe begins
14.8 billion years ago (14,800,000,000 years ago). In the early
Universe, there was only hydrogen, helium, and a trace of
lithium. Slap yourself on the shoulder. What you feel there is
a great deal more than those three elements. We are made
of carbon, hydrogen, oxygen, nitrogen, sulfur, phosphorus,
sodium, potassium, calcium, magnesium, iodine, iron,
manganese, molybdenum, and about a dozen other elements
found abundantly in the Earth's crust.

Where did all those elements come from? They came from
the cores of stars. That is correct. This is not a myth or a
legend, but is well-documented and well-understood science.
Our star – Sol – is busily converting hydrogen nuclei into
helium nuclei in its core. In about four or five billion years,
our star will run out of hydrogen in its core and will begin to

fuse helium nuclei into carbon nuclei. That is as far as our star will go. However, stars of much greater mass go much further, and the early Universe was populated by many super massive stars. Those stars go through cycles of fusing heavier and heavier elements, until they fuse iron. At that point, they blow up. You have undoubtedly heard the term "supernova." In such an explosion, all the elements of the periodic table are fused, right up to uranium, and they are scattered into interstellar space.

Over a period of hundreds of millions of years, interstellar clouds of gas and dust may become gravitationally unstable and collapse, forming new stars with planets. Now, however, the stars and their planetary systems have heavy elements – the type of elements of which we are made. Therefore, our Sun is a second or third generation star, and we are literally star children. A study of the manner in which the Universe has concocted the elements of which we are made, of the process by which the Earth formed, and of the way in which life has evolved can give us a special and delightful feeling about life. Life is a miraculous gift, and there are many ways in which we can enjoy and revel in that gift. Moreover, the longer we live, the longer we maintain our mental alertness, and the longer we maintain our physical fitness, the greater will be our joy and contentment in life.

So, read and re-read this book if necessary. Learn about all six types of exercise. Select the types of training that you can learn to enjoy and with which you can persist. If you believe that exercise is by necessity arduous and unpleasant, re-read chapter 3 and challenge that belief! You can learn to enjoy the sensations of physical activity! You really can! It is in our genetic heritage. Your life is important. Do everything you can to enhance it. Use the Principles for Happiness described in Chapter 16. Eat mostly healthy foods. Establish and maintain good sleep habits. ***And exercise!***

Glossary

Aerobic
Relating to, involving, or requiring free oxygen. Aerobic respiration is the process of producing cellular energy involving oxygen.

Agonist and antagonist muscles
Muscles must work together to produce different bodily movements, and a particular muscle's role may change depending on the movement. Two or more processes work together to produce a result greater than either could do alone. Agonist and antagonist muscles work in pairs and resist or counteract one another. An example of a pair of muscles working together can be seen in your arm. The muscle at the front of the arm is called the biceps muscle and the muscles at the back of the arm are called the triceps muscles. When the biceps muscle contracts, the triceps muscles relax. Agonists can be referred to as "prime movers," since they are primarily responsible for generating a specific movement. Other muscles, such as stabilizers, neutralizers, and fixators, help the effort by opposing unwanted movement or by helping to stabilize the joint.

Aerobic exercise
Aerobic exercise (popularly known as "cardio") is physical exercise that depends primarily on the aerobic energy-generating process. It refers to the use of oxygen to

adequately meet the body's energy demands. The first extensive research on aerobic exercise was conducted in the 1960s by Dr. Kenneth H. Cooper on over 5,000 U.S. Air Force personnel. Generally, light-to-moderate intensity activities that are sufficiently supported by aerobic metabolism can be performed for extended periods. A few examples of cardiovascular exercise are medium to long distance running/jogging, swimming, cycling, and brisk walking.

Anaerobic exercise

Anaerobic exercise is an activity in which muscular exertion is very great, and oxygen cannot be supplied to muscle fibers fast enough. It is used by athletes in non-endurance sports to promote strength, speed and power and by body builders to build muscle.

Antibody

An antibody is a blood protein produced in response to and counteracting a specific antigen. Antibodies combine chemically with and attempt to neutralize substances that the body recognizes as alien, such as bacteria and viruses.

Antigen

An antigen is any substance that causes your immune system to produce antibodies against it. An antigen may be a foreign substance from the environment, such as a chemical, bacterium, virus, or pollen.

Atrophy

See muscle atrophy.

Capillaries

Capillaries are the smallest of the body's blood vessels. They enable the exchange of water, oxygen, carbon dioxide, other nutrients, and waste substances between the bloodstream and the tissues surrounding them. Vigorous exercise causes the muscle tissue to adapt to the demand by creating new capillaries to supply the muscles with sufficient nutrients.

Cardiovascular System

The heart and circulatory system make up your cardiovascular system. Your heart is the pump that pushes blood to the organs, tissues, and cells of your body. Blood delivers oxygen and nutrients to the cells and removes the carbon dioxide and waste products.

Cardiovascular Exercise

This refers to activity that forces the lungs to oxygenate more blood and the heart to pump that oxygen-rich blood to the cells that need it. This type of exercise includes jogging, swimming, brink walking, and continuous action sports, and is often referred to as aerobic exercise. In colloquial speech, it is also simply called "cardio."

Concentric

This refers to the phase of an exercise in which the muscle shortens in length and develops tension to deliver force. For example, this would be the upward motion of hand-held weights in a biceps curl.

Eccentric

This refers to the phase of an exercise in which tension is maintained while a muscle is being lengthened. For example, this would be the downward motion of hand-held weights in a biceps curl exercise.

Epidemiology

Epidemiology is the science that studies the patterns, causes, and effects of health and disease conditions in defined populations. It is said to be the cornerstone of public health, and informs policy decisions and evidence-based practice by identifying risk factors for disease and targets for preventative healthcare.

Fatigue

For our purposes in this book, fatigue can be thought of as an activity-induced loss of ability to exert or maintain muscular force.

Free radical

A free radical is an atom, molecule, or ion that has unpaired valence electrons or an open electron shell, and therefore may be highly chemically reactive towards other substances.

Glial Cells

Glial cells are found in the brain, and there are far more glial cells in the brain than there are neurons. Glial cells have a variety of functions, including providing neuronal axons with the myelin sheaths that speed up nerve conduction.

Crucially, glial cells also store glycogen, and the steady supply of glycogen is essential for life.

Glycogen

Glycogen consists of long chains of glucose molecules, and is stored in the liver, muscles and brain cells. Glycogen is the body's fuel, and is used during muscular exertion. The greater the muscle glycogen stores prior to exercise, the longer the exercise time to exhaustion.

Golgi tendon reflex

The Golgi tendon reflex is a reaction of the body to reduce the chance of a muscle tear. Skeletal muscle contractions cause the agonist muscle to simultaneously lengthen and relax. This reflex is also called the inverse myotatic reflex, because it is the inverse of the stretch reflex, which typically occurs first.

Homeostasis

Homeostasis is the property of the body by which variables are regulated with the purpose of maintaining stable internal conditions. For example, our bodies have systems to regulate temperature, blood sugar, blood oxygen and the balance between acidity and alkalinity, as well as many others.

Immune System

The immune system is the body's defense against infectious organisms and other invaders. Through the immune response, the immune system attacks organisms and substances that can cause disease.

Muscle atrophy

Muscle atrophy is a decrease in the mass of the muscle, either partial or complete. It is most commonly experienced when persons suffer temporary inactivity such as being restricted in movement or confined to bed.

Myotatic Reflex

The stretch reflex (myotatic reflex) is a muscle contraction in response to stretching within the muscle. It is a reflex that provides automatic regulation of skeletal muscle length.

Osteoporosis

Osteoporosis is a medical condition in which bones become brittle and fragile from loss of tissue, typically because of hormonal changes, inactivity, or deficiency of calcium or vitamin D.

Procedural memory

Procedural memory is the memory of "how to" – of procedures. This is an unconscious type of memory. How to type, to play a piece on the piano, to turn your baseball glove to backhand a ground ball, and to do a push-up or a crunch are all examples of procedural memory.

Proprioception

Proprioception is the unconscious perception of movement and spatial orientation arising from stimuli within the body itself. In humans, these stimuli are detected by vision, by nerves within the body itself, and by the semicircular canals of the inner ear.

Regimen
An organized course of exercise, diet, or medical treatment for the promotion or restoration of health.

Regiment
A military unit with a commanding officer and divided into companies, squadrons, or battalions. *This word has nothing to do with this book. Do not confuse this with the word "regimen."*

Tao
(Pronounced "Dow") Tao means "the way." Taoism is the original religion of China, with roots going back over five thousand years.

References

Amen, Daniel G., MD. *Magnificent at Any Age*. New York: Harmony Books, 2008.

Anderson, Bob. *Stretching*. Bolinas, CA: Shelter Publications, 2000.

Bailey, Covert. *Smart Exercise: Burning Fat, Getting Fit*. Boston: Houghton Mifflin. 1994.

Bean, Constance A. *The Better Back Book*. New York: William Morrow, 1989.

Benson, Herbert. *The Relaxation Response*.

Blahnik, Jay. *Full-Body Flexibility*, Second Edition. Champaign, Illinois: Human Kinetics, 2011.

Baechle, Thomas, Earle, Roger. *Weight Training: Steps to Success*, Third Edition. Champaign, Illinois: Human Kinetics, 2006.

Broad, William. *The Science of Yoga: The Risks and Rewards*. New York: Simon and Schuster, 2012.

Capouya, John. *Real Men Do Yoga*. Deerfield Beach, FL: Health Communications, 2003.

Chia, Mantak and Li, Juan. *The Inner Structure of Tai Chi*. Huntington, New York: Healing Tao Books. 1996.

Dahm, Diane and Smith, Jay. *Mayo Clinic: Fitness for Everybody*. New York: Kensington, 2005.

Davis, Jennifer et al., "Challenges with cost-utility analyses of behavioural interventions among older adults at risk for dementia," *British Journal of Sports Medicine*, 40.20 (October 2015), 1343.

Delavier, Frederic, Clemenceau, Jean-Pierre and Gundill, Michael. *Delavier's Stretching Anatomy*. Champaign, Illinois: Human Kinetics, 2010.

Doeser, Linda. *The Yoga Directory*. New York: Metro Books, 2003.

Emily Zhao, Michael Tranovich & Vonda Wright, "The Role of Mobility as a protective factor of cognitive functioning in aging adult," *Sports Health*, 2014, Jan. 6(1), 63-69.

Fenton, Peter and Galante, Lawrence. *Wisdom of Tai Chi: Ancient Secrets to Health and Harmony*. Lincolnwood, Illinois: Publications International, 1998.

Fielding, Deborah. *The Healthy Back Exercise Book*. Barnes & Noble Books, 2001.

Franklin, Eric. *Relax Your Neck; Liberate Your Shoulders*. Hightstown, NJ: Princeton Book Co., 2002.

Frantzis, Bruce, *Tai Chi: Health for Life*, Berkeley, CA: Blue Snake Books, 2003.

Harvard Medical School, "Glycemic index and glycemic load for 100+ foods," *Harvard Health Publication*, February 2015.

Hodgkin, Dean. *Physiology and Fitness*. Chantilly, VA: The Great Courses, 2012.

Iyengar, B.K.S. *YOGA: The Path to Holistic Health*. London: Dorling Kindersley, 2001.

Jacobson, Edmund. *Progressive Relaxation*. 1934

Karter, Karon. *The Core Strength Workout*. Gloucester, MA: Fair Winds Press, 2004.

Kirsch, David. *Sound Mind, Sound Body*. New York: Rodale, Inc., 2002.

Lee, Cyndi. *May I Be Happy: A Memoir of Love, Yoga and Changing My Mind*. New York: Dutton, 2013.

McFarlane, Stewart. *The Complete Book of Tai Chi*. New York: DK Publishing. 1997.

Manocchia, Pat. *Anatomy of Strength Training: The 5 Essential Exercises.* San Diego: Thunder Bay Press, 2010.

Martin, Suzanne, *Stretching: The stress-free way to stay supple, keep fit and exercise safely*. New York: DK Publishing, 2005.

Mayo Clinic Staff, "Healthy dirt: Do you follow dietary guidelines?" *Nutrition and Healthy Eating*, Feb 2013.

Meeks, Sara. *Walk Tall: An Exercise Program for Prevention & Treatment of Back Pain, Osteoporosis and the Postural Changes of Aging*. Gainesville, FL: Triad Publishing, 2010.

Metzl, Jordan. *The Exercise Cure: A Doctor's Prescription for Better Health & Longer Life*. New York: Rodale, 2013.

Nelson, Arnold and Kokkonen, Jouko. ***Stretching Anatomy***. Champaign, Illinois: Human Kinetics, 2007.

O'Connor, Herring and Corvalle, "Mental health benefits of strength training in adults," ***American Journal of Lifestyle Medicine***, 2010, 4 (5), 377-396.

Osterweil, Neil, "Beef up your knowledge of protein and good dietary sources," ***WebMD***, 2004.

Peterson, Gunnar. ***G-Force: The Ultimate Guide to Your Best Body Ever.*** New York: Harper Collins, 2005.

Roman Meeusen, "Exercise, Nutrition and the Brain," ***Sports Medicine***, May 2014, Vol. 44, Supplement 1, pp. 47-56.

Rosenfeld, Arthur. ***Tai Chi: The Perfect Exercise***. Boston: Da Capo Press, 2013.

Schiffmann, Erich. ***Yoga: The Spirit and Practice of Moving Into Stillness***. New Yprk: Pocket Books, 1996.

Sivananda ***Yoga Vedanta Center, Yoga: Your Home Practice Companion***. New York: DK Publishing, 2010.

Tucker, Paul. ***Tai Chi: Flowing Movements for Harmony and Balance***. New York: Lorenz Books, 1997.

Wayne, Peter & Fuerst, Mark. T***he Harvard Medical School Guide to Tai Chi***. Boston: Chambala, 2013.

Westcott, Wayne. ***Building Strength & Stamina***, Second Edition. Champaign, Illinois: Human Kinetics, 2003.

Worby, Cynthia. *The Everything Yoga Book*. Avon, Massachusetts: Adams Media. 2002.

Yu, Tricia. *Tai Chi: Mind and Body*. New York: Dorling Kindersley, 2003.

About the Author

Dr. Michael Slavit is a psychologist in private practice. He is Board Certified in Behavioral and Cognitive Psychology by the American Board of Professional Psychology. However, the "credential" of which he is most proud is the confidence his patients have in him.

Dr. Slavit received his Bachelor of Arts degree in psychology from Brown University, his Master's Degree in counseling from the University of Rhode Island, and his Ph.D. in Counseling Psychology from the University of Texas at Austin. His main areas of expertise as a psychotherapist are stress management, overcoming depression, Attention Deficit Hyperactivity Disorder, Positive Psychology, grief and bereavement, relationship issues, and health / fitness / weight.

Dr. Slavit has taught psychology, counseling and personal development courses at four colleges and universities. His interests include science, writing, fitness, swimming, hiking and kayaking. In addition to **Embracing Fitness**, his books include:

- **Your Life: An Owner's Guide**
- **Lessons from Desiderata**
- **Train Your Wandering Mind: Cope with ADHD**, and
- **Cure Your Money Ills: Improve Your Self-esteem through Personal Budgeting**

Dr. Slavit has an avid interest in science, and he has works in progress, including books entitled:

- *A Brief History of the Universe, The Earth and Life*, and
- *My Life as a T Rex*

Embrace Life

Embrace Fitness